g41 Green house salad

"Dear Cora..."

By Cora Holmes

In this, her second
book, Cora answers
questions from
readers of her first.

Contents

Editor: Mike Beno
Assistant Editors: John Schroeder,
Kristine Krueger, Henry de Fiebre
Art Director: Gail Engeldahl
Art Associate: Maribeth Greinke
Photography: Julie Habel, Milt Holmes
Photo Coordinator: Trudi Bellin
Publisher: Roy J. Reiman

© 1997 Reiman Publications, L.P.
5400 S. 60th St., Greendale WI 53129

Country Books
International Standard Book Number:
0-89821-195-6

Library of Congress Catalog Card Number:
96-72182

All rights reserved. Printed in U.S.A.

For additional copies of this book or
information on other books, write:
Country Books, P.O. Box 990, Greendale WI 53129.
Credit card orders call toll-free 1-800/558-1013.

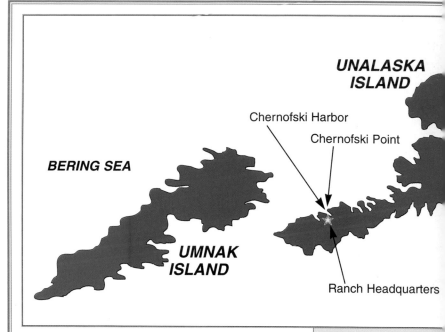

UNALASKA
ISLAND

Chernofski Harbor

Chernofski Point

BERING SEA

UMNAK
ISLAND

Ranch Headquarters

Aleutian Islands

UNALASKA is part of the island chain that stretches 1,100 miles from mainland Alaska into the Bering Sea. At Chernofski Sheep Ranch, Milt and Cora Holmes live isolated, peaceful and happy, 85 miles from the nearest town. The only way to reach their 152,000-acre ranch is by boat or floatplane.

utch Harbor

Unalaska
Village

DURING World War II, the Aleutian archipelago was strategically important to the United States, which repelled Japanese attacks there. The city of Dutch Harbor, for example, was bombed. U.S. military personnel set up bases at Chernofski Bay and on the neighboring island of Umnak. Today, Milt and Cora are genuinely grateful to those who saved their island. Cora regularly corresponds with veterans of the Aleutian campaign, and some of their letters are included in this book.

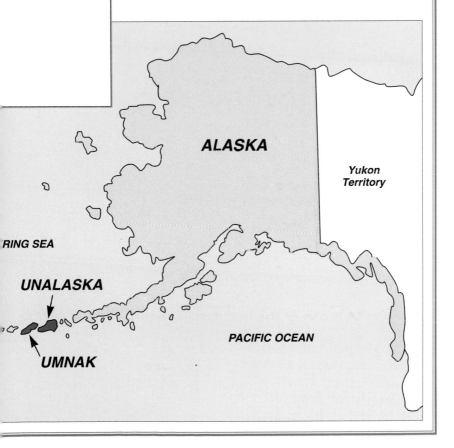

ALASKA

Yukon
Territory

RING SEA

UNALASKA

UMNAK

PACIFIC OCEAN

FOREWORD

By Roy Reiman, Publisher

IN 1989, the readers of *Country* magazine first met Cora Holmes. Her letters described her family's life on a 152,000-acre sheep ranch on Unalaska Island in the Aleutian chain off the coast of Alaska.

The island is so isolated that Cora and husband Milt sometimes never see another person for months. They receive mail only four or five times a year...but the beauty, the challenge and the pace of the place are such that they never want to leave.

Cora's magazine writings described the wild horse herds on the island...how she and Milt order supplies once every 2 years and have them shipped from Seattle by freight boat...how they heat their home with coal left by the military in 1945...how they make a living from marketing wool, beef, lamb and tanned pelts from winter trapping.

By giving readers such insights into her life, Cora simply made them more curious. Hundreds of people from all across the country wrote to her (and to us here at Reiman Publications) asking to know more.

Folks Liked Her Book

This inspired Cora to write her first book, *Good-Bye, Boise...Hello, Alaska*. It was published in 1994, and some 40,000 people have purchased the book so far. By any measure, that's mighty successful.

When Cora received her royalty check, she wrote us: "Milt and I discussed how to make a difference for veterans who served in the Aleutians during the war. We wanted a personal gift that said, 'Thank you for saving Chernofski Sheep Ranch for us.'

"Since we could not include everyone, we chose two whose letters had touched our hearts. One man is ill with liver cancer, yet he made the effort to write and tell us how cold the Bering Sea was when he waded up to his neck with a full field pack in the dark hours before the invasion of Kiska.

Back to Chernofski

"The other is a man who wrote about his dream of coming back to Chernofski and spending one more night in the bunker on the point across the bay from the ranch where he spent his lonely service months."

In short, Cora donated half her earnings to people she'd never met. The Holmeses are not rich people.

"Out here, our luxuries are free—clean air, privacy, unlimited personal freedom. But necessity makes me keep half of it," Cora wrote. "Supplies cost money, and nearly all of ours were destroyed when a boat ran into a storm a year ago."

It's not surprising that Cora's readers keep asking to know more about this unselfish and kind person, and the unique life she lives.

This book, *"Dear Cora..."*, is her follow-up to *Good-Bye, Boise...Hello, Alaska*. It gives those ever-curious readers an even deeper look into the Holmeses' life.

Cora selected some of the most-asked questions from her correspondence and provides insightful, enjoyable answers.

I hope all of Cora's readers enjoy this, her second book. We certainly enjoyed working with her to publish it.

Acknowledgments

AGAIN, I want to thank Roy Reiman and his staff for their help and interest.

As always, I'm forever indebted to Milt, this time for eating peanut butter and jelly sandwiches instead of suppers.

I want to thank my sons, Chuck and Randall, for accepting with grace the notoriety I escaped when *Good-Bye, Boise...Hello, Alaska* hit the bookstore in Unalaska Village.

A special thank-you to our *Country* working vacationer, Anna Buterbaugh, for sorting and copying letters, besides doing a great many dishes.

But most of all, I want to thank all you *Country* readers who enjoyed my book enough to write and tell me so. This one's for you.

Cora Holmes
Chernofski Sheep Ranch, Unalaska Island

Introduction

Whatever happened to Peep-Sheep? How did Chernofski get its name? Are you and Milt ever going to retire?

I wrote *Good-Bye, Boise...Hello, Alaska* for all the *Country* readers who asked to know more about the way we lived, how we found our isolated home and why we wanted to live this way.

Judging from the letters pouring in since the book was published, instead of answering such questions, it merely raised more!

With Chuck's and Randall's permission, Milt's help, Roy Reiman's encouragement, Julie Habel's photography and your continued interest, I'm giving you a deeper look into our lives by answering those questions most often asked when Milt and I pore over the sacks of mail that arrive here by boat or floatplane every few months.

When the first planeload of letters from *Country* readers arrived on our beach, we were pleased and surprised that so many people enjoyed reading about our life enough to write and tell us.

But we were puzzled, too. What piqued so much interest in this isolated, hostile environment and the family who loves it? Last night at the supper table, we read a letter from Beverly Daffron of Pennington Gap, Virginia. Her letter holds some clues about the origins of this curiosity:

I'm reading your book and enjoying it so much I can't put it down. Since I feel I know you, perhaps I should tell you a little about myself. I'm a 34-year-old homemaker in Pennington Gap, Virginia, a small town of 2,000.

My husband, Greg, is the operating room director at a hospital. He's a kind man and a hard worker. We have two girls, Jennifer and Catherine. I'm a former teacher, and I'm educating our children at home. We enjoy home-schooling very much.

Even though we aren't in a remote area like you are, I can relate to your stories about teaching kids at home.

As I read your book, I wonder just what makes your life-style so appealing. I think it's the peace and quiet and simplicity that reaches out to us. For sure, it's a lot more glamorous to read about lives like yours than to live them.

I think there's something in us that's tired of this rat-race existence and wants to get back to basics. Of course, that's easier said than done, but we crave it anyway.

Sometimes I wonder if God meant for life to become this complicated. He has been good to our family and I'm thankful for His blessings. Compared with most people's lives today, ours is relatively uncomplicated.

Cora, may God bless you and Milt. You are most fortunate to have found such a life.

I'm writing this update for Beverly and every *Country* reader who wanted to know more. Most of the questions in this book have been attributed to the person who wrote and asked. They're identified at the end of their questions.

Other questions were posed by so many people that I've attributed them to no one individual, rather than singling out only one person.

I've tried to be cheerful, funny and honest, but now and then, I opened up a vein. I hope you enjoy it!

THE GOOD LIFE. As readers familiar with the Holmeses' life at Chernofski know, there aren't many days when Cora can take time for a quiet read or to share a cup of coffee with Milt. The boats, the family's most important tools, need constant attention. And when Chuck and Randall were still home, there were horses, sheep and cattle to tend.

FRIENDS AND FAMILY. With only each other to count on, the Holmeses have managed well on their remote Aleutian Island ranch. Cora, Milt and the boys learned to live, love, work and laugh together.

Are You Ever Going to Retire?

Now that your book is doing so well, are you going to move some-place warmer and just relax and enjoy yourselves?
—Pauline and Dudge Yost, Ten Sleep, Wyoming

THIS IS the most frequent question we hear—it surfaces in many letters. Pauline and Dudge took it a step further and paid us this supreme compliment: "You folks would make good neighbors."

I'll admit that if any place could tempt us away from Cher-nofski, it just may be Wyoming, with its wide-open spaces, sparse population and 80-mph winds.

No matter how hard life is here, we love it and have no plans to leave our ranch. We can't imagine another place in the

WOODSHED LESSON. When we can't do this, the boys will come help, but for now, we still enjoy physical labor. Although the woodpile looks daunting, Milt split it all and I stored it in the woodshed in one afternoon. Chuck and Randall used to think Milt had some magic formula until he showed them how to use a splitting maul and wedge. "It's simple," he told them. "You don't have to swing with all your strength; let the weight of the maul do the work. Two medium whacks are better than one power swing, and if you miss the wedge, you don't break the maul handle."

world as relaxing. Storms and solitude don't frighten us like freeways and malls with their confusing exits and entrances.

But the years are piling up and we can't ride horses anymore. Since sheep are our first love, we are parting with our cattle and downsizing our flock enough to manage with dogs on foot.

Milton is 73 years old, and when I ask him about retiring, he always looks surprised and says, "Me, retire? Why? I can still go like I'm 50...just takes me longer."

SHAKE-MAKER. In the summer of 1992, we put on a new shake roof. Milt hopes he doesn't have to do this again, not because of the difficulty in sawing, splitting and installing the shakes, but because a flawless cedar log doesn't float into our harbor every year. The one he made these shakes from drifted ashore in Wood Cove, 2-1/2 miles from headquarters, 13 years ago. All four of us spent days sawing and hauling it overland to the ranch. When the weather and sea conditions allowed Milt to take his small boat out of the harbor, he and the boys skiffed to the cove and brought boatloads home. Besides the shakes he has made for both roof and outside walls, Milt finished a room in the original ranch house, which is now used as a guest house, with rough board-and-batten cedar paneling. He reluctantly made me some picture frames, but he's hoarding the rest.

RADIO MAN. When Milt can no longer climb the antenna for repairs, we'll retire...our radio. Here he is (above) repairing the antenna after a storm last fall when the stabilizing wires weren't enough to hold it. The smokestack to the right is also a frequent casualty to storms, despite Milt's efforts to tie it down. On these clear fall days, our only visible contact with civilization is an occasional contrail from a high-flying airplane. But on the ground, our contact with past civilization, in the form of abandoned military equipment (below), affords Milt a place to salvage some items he can put to use around the ranch.

Sounds Familiar

What does "Chernofski" mean?

OUR HARBOR'S unusual name sparks a lot of interest. Queries regularly come from people of Polish or Russian ancestry who say it has a familiar ring. Others are merely curious at the odd spelling, but Milt and I got a good chuckle when Dr. James Dacus of Liberty, South Carolina asked because, "My mailman wants to know".

Legend has it that during the 1700s, when Russia discovered the Aleutian Islands, the first man to sail into the harbor was Captain Tchernof. The harbor and settlement there were named in his honor—the village of Tchernof, or Tchernofsky.

The "T" disappeared over the years and the more common spelling uses "ski", but we still see it ended "sky" in books. One old map identifies it as *Chernovi*.

Tcherno means "black" in the Russian language. So, roughly, Chernofski translates to the "Village of Black", or "Black's Village"—not nearly so romantic sounding as Chernofski. I think we'll stick with the Russian version.

Before Russian contact, the islanders had no written language. But they had a rich and varied oral one. From a translation of writings by the Russian priest Veniaminov, I discovered the original name of the bay was *Ikalga*.

According to Veniaminov, Chernofski was the poorest village on the island in the early 1800s, having only four *yurtas* (homes) and 44 inhabitants.

Bob Marshall

LINK TO THE PAST. This Russian Orthodox church in Unalaska Village has recently undergone restoration on its onion domes. It reminds us of the Russian heritage that links Chernofski to the past, even without the original 'T'.

Sounds Like Milt Is a Wonderful Man

I love spending time with my husband. Sounds like Milt is a wonderful man. What kinds of fun things do you two do? What other kinds of things has he made for you?
—Elizabeth Denny, Garner, North Carolina

I KNEW Elizabeth and I were kindred spirits when she said she loved spending time with her husband.

The time I spend doing fun things with Milt is precious and scarce. Our habits of daily living keep us both busy in separate places most of the time.

Often he leaves the house after breakfast and I don't see him again until dark. So when he suggests beachcombing,

ROCKY BEACHES. This one's not far from where I found the mahogany timber. As inhospitable as these rocks look, we still find glass floats resting in their crevices. The tall U-shaped rock formation in the background with the grass growing on top is a bald eagle's nest.

which is our favorite leisure-time activity, I drop everything and go with him.

No matter how often we've done it, beachcombing kindles a child's Easter-egg-hunt anticipation in both of us. We just know there's something wonderful around the next headland—like the time I found a 10-foot mahogany timber washed up with other logs. It was so big and heavy we had to wait months for Chuck's next visit so he could help us get it home.

Since it was my discovery, Milt said I could use it for whatever I wanted—a big concession in our treeless environment, where every stick of hardwood we find is hoarded for boat repairs.

I had my heart set on a curio cabinet I'd seen in a catalog. Even though I knew it was a lot to expect with our limited tools, I asked Milt to make it.

The most sophisticated equipment in his shop was an old Sears circular saw with a 2-inch blade. Since the timber was 6 inches square, it was a challenge.

Undaunted, Milt hand-sawed off a chunk, then ripped 2 inches into it on both sides with the power saw. Then he clamped it in his vise, lined up a handsaw with the cuts and sawed through the remaining wood. He repeated this until he had eight boards, each 1/4 inch thick and roughly the same size.

Next he used his horseshoe rasp to even out the surface before sanding each board with increasing grits of sandpaper until the finish satisfied him.

Making the cabinet was the easy part. In no time, he fashioned a beautiful wall cabinet with scrollwork and filigree designs on the sides using only a handsaw and wood chisels.

I love it. After it was on the wall and filled with small treasures from the attic, such as old spice cans and medicine bottles, I stopped to admire it a dozen times a day.

"It's perfect," I told him, thinking about the remaining timber and envisioning a spice rack, bookshelf and picture frames, all the same glossy material. "What will you make out of the rest of it?"

He didn't even pause to think. "A fence post comes to mind," he replied.

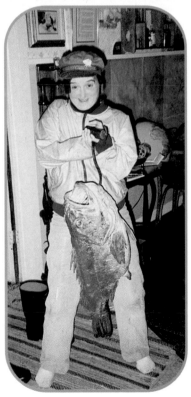

BEACHCOMBING BONANZA. The one glass Japanese fishing float I'm holding (above) made this day of beachcombing worthwhile. We also collected some kindling, which we carry in the plastic baskets, and some fishing buoys (behind the tracked Ferret), which made good trade items with the boat crews. Milt can't hike long distances anymore, so the track machine is a handy vehicle to haul home all our treasures.

FRIED OR BOILED? This huge red snapper I'm struggling to heft (left) was a gift from a visiting fishing boat. We'd never be able to catch monsters like this on a pole. We'd be towed out to sea the way Randall once was in his raft.

WOODWORKING. Milt's skill with tools came in handy (right) when he went to Unalaska to help Randall and Jennifer set up housekeeping in a World War II cabana.

HELPMATE. Most of the time, daily chores keep Milt and me in separate places during the day. So the times we can do fun things together, like beachcombing, are precious. Milt also does his share of work around the stove (above) ...and there's nothing like an impromptu massage (right) for getting out the kinks after a hard day.

Whatever Happened to Peep-Sheep?

I once had a pet lamb as a little girl and I haven't eaten lamb since; I guess I'd starve at your place. —Martha Lookenbill
York, Pennsylvania

MARTHA and husband Larry love animals so much that when their yellow Lab, "Marigold", brought them a tiny furry bundle one evening at twilight, Larry laboriously climbed a tree in their yard and deposited it back in the resident squirrel nest.

All was well until the next morning, when Marigold brought another furry bundle, which they identified in full light as a baby rabbit.

Larry scrambled back up that tree and rescued the first rabbit from among the baby squirrels, and with Marigold's help, returned both to their nest.

When I read this incident in Martha's letter around the supper table, it gave us such a good feeling I wanted everyone to hear it. The squirrels and rabbits in the Lookenbills' yard are indeed lucky they enjoy the same kind of protection my pet sheep have.

Although we raise sheep for both meat and wool, any bum lamb we save becomes a family member. "Peep" was the first. He lived a full happy life and brought on his own demise by being a pig. He loved sneaking into the chicken house to gobble their feed. He eventually caught circling disease from the chicken droppings and we couldn't save him.

He has since been followed by "Fred", "Wes", "Woody", "Toughie", "Jasper" and, finally, "Treasure". But Peep will always have a special place in our hearts. Whenever I see our current pet frolicking across the yard, I remember Peep-Sheep and how brave he was.

ANOTHER "BUM". I found "Jasper" abandoned by his mother 3 miles from headquarters. He is the lamb Julie Habel photographed for "Good-Bye, Boise". He is now full grown and has given us 9 pounds of wool.

STEEP PEEP. Whenever we went anywhere, "Peep-Sheep" came with us. On November 30, 1987, we had an earthquake and headed for higher ground (above) just in case it caused a tidal wave. Peep didn't even have to be coaxed. We climbed to 300 feet. Snow-covered Mt. Aspid is in the background.

PACKER PEEP. Peep was our first pet, and I'll always have a special fond memory of him and all the wool he gave us. He still lives on in the sweaters and mittens I made from his fleece. But my best memory of him is that of a good friend and companion. Here he is beachcombing with me; the pack he wore carried my small treasures home.

BARNYARD BUNCH (above) includes "Jasper", "Barney", "Buck", "Shorty" and "Friendly". Besides being fun to watch, they pay their way by helping train sheepdogs and cow horses.

WELL DRESSED. One way my pets earn their keep is by producing hand spinning wool. As "Tar Baby" models at left, we put coats on them to keep out moss and sand. They don't like clothes, and it's a dreadful job to keep them dressed.

Can We Meet Jennifer?

Greetings from the Texas Panhandle. I've just finished reading your book and I can see why you love it there. I was disappointed there was no picture of Randall's wife in the book.
—Pat Hardy, Perryton, Texas

MANY of you already know Jennifer through pictures in *Country* magazine and personal correspondence with us. We are so proud of her and happy to have her as part of our family.

Randall and Jennifer met in Unalaska Village one summer. She was the daughter of a visiting minister and Randall was doing a construction apprenticeship for a local contractor.

Their romance began in a typical Aleutian fashion. She was walking in the rain and he gave her a lift.

WELCOMING JENNIFER. Milton and I made the long, difficult trip to California to be a part of their wedding. Randall wanted Milton to be his best man. "I respect you more than anyone and I want you to stand up with me, please," he said. They asked Milt to dress in black, cowboy hat and all. Everyone who attended thought he was a rabbi.

WEDDING PORTRAIT. Randall and Jennifer were married in Jennifer's father's church in Eureka, California.

WILD RIDE.
Jennifer gets ready to ride "Velvet" (right), one of Randall's mustangs.

BOO! Randall and Jennifer celebrate Halloween by trick-or-treating at the main house (left). They lived next door in the bunkhouse. Having them here all one winter brightened up the short days.

HONEYMOON?
Jennifer helps push cattle through the chute on a blustery fall day (right).

PIE TIME. Jennifer is an accomplished artist and looks like a fashion model, but she took to ranch life the minute she got off the plane. The first winter she spent here, she learned to cook by reading my cookbooks and practicing. Here she is making apple pies (right) from scratch to help feed 16 guests.

HAPPY FAMILY. Jennifer's parents are beside her, and her brother and sister are kneeling in front. Randall's smile tells it all.

How Did You Lose Your Hand?

What courage it took for you to move to the Aleutians. How hard your family worked under such trying conditions. My heart goes out to you, Cora, and the extra burden you had to overcome with the loss of your hand. —*Elizabeth Endres*
Kendall Park, New Jersey

AS AN ARTIST, Elizabeth knows how important hands are. But more important, as grandmother to Laura, who became a quadriplegic at age 17, she knows about courage, because she and her whole family rallied around Laura, supporting and encouraging her.

Today Laura, at 39, is a computer expert with a satisfying career, and I'm alive to tell her story because my big family did the same for me.

I had a rare sarcoma, quick to spread, and deadly. And I had waited 5 months before coming out from Chernofski because I thought the lump beside my thumb was caused by breaking a blood vessel while I helped Milt and Chuck butcher steers.

The minute the surgeon told me, I knew I was dead. I could see it in his eyes. Even with amputation and industrial doses of chemotherapy, my chances of surviving longer than a year were less then 25%.

In a strange numb state, sort of like I had forgotten how to breathe, I consented to the surgery only if the disease hadn't spread to my lymph system.

When I woke up in the recovery room without my right hand, I knew I had a chance to live, and everyone I loved made sure I had a lot of reasons.

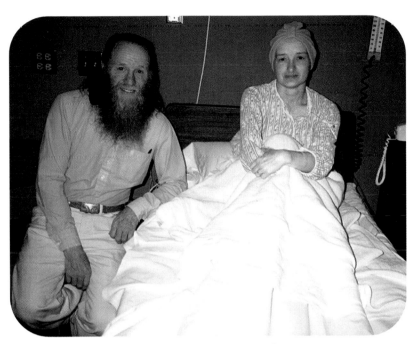

BEDSIDE MANNER. Milt dropped everything to take care of me through the entire 6 months of chemotherapy. He even spent every night in the hospital (above), sleeping on a cot beside my bed.

HOME CARE. Daniel Lopez (right), a friend and registered nurse I worked with before going to Chernofski, offered to take care of me between hospitalizations. Milt and I lived in the basement at Daniel's house for half a year, where Daniel and his wife, Hilary, also a nurse, saved my life many times.

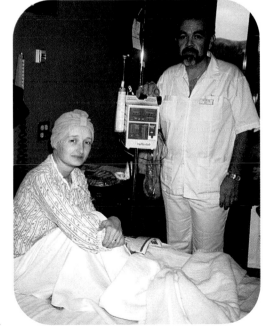

BIRTHDAY BOY. Chuck spent his 21st birthday beside my bed. But Hilary Kate, Dan Lopez's daughter, made sure he had a birthday cake (left).

MOM AND MILT. My mother and Milt (right, in non-matching aprons) did a lot of experimenting in Mom's Cascade, Idaho kitchen, trying to tempt my non-existent appetite. The night before the surgery, I joined the family in my sister Doris' Boise, Idaho home (below) in making Easter decorations. I found that keeping busy helped.

HOME AGAIN. The day after I got home, I visited with our Icelandic ballerina friend, Helga (above). Our smiles tell how happy we were.

FRIENDS INDEED. Our friends in Unalaska Village gave Milt and me a dinner party on our return (below). Besides helping out at the ranch wherever they could, these good people pooled their resourses and bought me my first artificial hand.

INSPIRATION. Elizabeth Endres' artwork (left) helps me look forward to being 89. The photo of Elizabeth, her daughter Gloria and granddaughter Laura (below) hangs above my desk where I am inspired every time I look at it.

SISTERLY LOVE. My sisters, Doris and Virginia (right), drove me to the Boise River, where I loved to walk.

MAN OF THE RANCH. At 17, Randall had the lonely task of running the ranch while we were gone (below). It was a big job, but he did it.

Single-Handed Housekeeping

You had to make quite an adjustment after losing your hand. How do you do household chores? —*Doris Johnson*
Lyons, New York

DORIS KNOWS how much work is involved in running a house, because she cans and freezes vegetables from her own garden and raises calves.

Two hands are nice, of course, but one does most of the work and the other acts as one side of a "vise". I learned that 2 weeks after my amputation, when I attempted a counted cross-stitch picture and realized I couldn't thread a needle.

After handing the needle to Milt several times, I said, "I wish I could do this myself."

"I don't mind," he answered, "But when I'm not here, just do this." He jabbed the needle into my denim jeans just above the knee. "Try that."

It worked! My first vise. In the months that followed, I discovered a great many vises. Teeth, for instance, or under my arm. Knees work, too.

Milton modified my kitchen and spinning tools to fit my hook so I could use my right arm as the primary worker. This accomplishment encouraged me so much that after I mastered sweeping, mopping and washing dishes, I went on to bigger and better things.

After reminding me every time he caught me pounding nails with my fiberglass arm that it made an expensive hammer, Milt modified an old hammer head so it would screw into my hook socket.

Having mastered hammering, cooking, cleaning, typing and even spinning, I'm embarrassed to admit I still can't write with my left hand so anyone can read it—even after 10 years. Whenever I write Chuck a check, he just shakes his head and teases, "I bet I'm the only guy at the bank whose check looks like it was written by a second grader."

SINGLE-HANDED COOKING. Cooking a black cod dinner for 16 means I have to start the preparations the minute I finish breakfast. I have to allow for mopping up spills and other unforeseen accidents. One thing that helps is a World War II-vintage, heavy-duty can opener that Milt's son Val found in an abandoned military building. It's bolted to the kitchen counter and is the only can opener I can use with one hand.

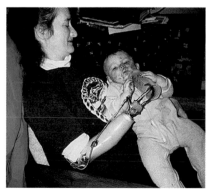

LICKIN' GOOD. After licking out a cake dish, our little friend Taylor doesn't care how his bottle is held.

STITCHING AGAIN. When I discovered the "fanny frame" (right), I was able to get back to my needlework.

BACK TO THE WHEEL. The day I got home from Idaho, Nov. 5, 1986, I sat down at my wheel and made some very lumpy yarn (above). Milt modified my hand carders so I could prepare wool for spinning. When I had a skein, I began knitting (left).

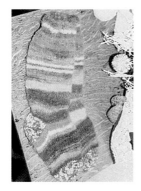

SANTA SOCKS. I made Randall these socks for Christmas 1986.

CARD SHARP. With the carders modified by Milt, I can prepare the wool. By clamping one carder to the table (above), I can pull the other one across it and straighten out the fibers.

TAKE A NUMBER. Since I could only feed one of them at a time, the calves learned to wait their turn (left). Like little Taylor, they didn't mind how their bottles were held.

Can We Visit Your Greenhouse?

Lots of us would like to hear what is being produced in that greenhouse. —Frances Camizzi, Cedar Rapids, Iowa

NICE WORDS from Frances, who read my book and thoughtfully lent it to a friend whose health gave him a need for other things to think about.

Judging by the amount of seeds that arrive in letters from *Country* readers, everyone loves the greenhouse. It is a favorite job for working vacationers and visiting family members to plant and nurture those seeds in the one building on the ranch that gets truly hot inside.

Even my 82-year-old mother wanted her turn during her 6-month visit here 5 years ago. She came in the spring when it was much too early to plant. Still, she wanted to enjoy the sunshine coming through the glass from the first day on.

Even being March, it was wonderfully warm inside. But I cautioned her about staying too long when I opened the door and showed her around. She assured me she'd only stay a few

minutes, so I left her puttering around in the bare beds and returned to my own chores.

When she didn't appear in 10 minutes, I glanced through the living room window into the greenhouse. I saw she was putting on her scarf and gloves, so I went back to my

PEA-PICKER. I have to restrain myself, or I'd eat every pea as soon as it was ripe. I have to save some to go with the potatoes you see cascading out of their bed. The potatoes taste wonderful creamed with those fresh peas...if there are any of them left!

HOT SPOT. The greenhouse (above, with the Ferret parked in front) is everyone's favorite spot. Even on an overcast day, like this one, it will be warm inside.

FREE AT LAST. Finally out of the greenhouse, Grandma Gorley cuddled a couple of baby chicks to celebrate her recent freedom.

dishwashing. After 30 minutes, I looked again and she was sitting with mittened hands folded across her lap. Perhaps she just needs more time to soak up the sun, I thought, and went on to sweep the kitchen.

But when another half hour had elapsed and I finished kneading my bread dough, the last morning chore, I decided enough was enough. She had mentioned baking cookies and playing Scrabble before Chuck and Milt came in for lunch.

I hurried out to remind her...and discovered I had locked her in!

Grandma Gorley's Greenhouse Salad
(Like her grandmother used to make)
Ingredients:
  Leaf lettuce—any variety—washed and chilled
  Dill pickle juice
  Granulated sugar
  Cinnamon
Arrange lettuce in rows on platter until you have a nice mound. Cut through mound with scissors every 2 inches so the lettuce is in bite-size pieces. Drizzle dill pickle juice over lettuce. Sprinkle liberally with sugar and cinnamon.

Colors from the Countryside

I'm interested in dyeing material, and I read that you make dyes. Could you send me some recipes for different colors?
—Lisa Spegal, Newport, Kentucky

ONE PASTIME more satisfying than spinning wool from a sheep you raised is picking wildflowers from the same hills that fed your animal and using them to dye the yarn a natural color.

While many Aleutian wildflowers yield a color, most are shades of green, yellow, or brown. However, the native lichens that thrive in our clean air give intense hues ranging from purple to ivory.

The Way I Do It:

1. Wash yarn in detergent and 120° water.
2. Rinse, drain and store wet in a cool place for 1 week.
3. Mordant yarn by adding 2 tablespoons regular powdered alum and 1 teaspoon cream of tartar to a gallon of cool water, then put in yarn and simmer for 1 hour.
4. Cool overnight in mordant; drain and add to cool dye bath.
5. Cool in dye bath; rinse until the water remains clear.
6. Dry in shade.
7. Make something beautiful!

NATURAL BEAUTY. This handspun yarn was dyed a variety of ways, with Aleutian plants, lichens and various food colorings. The reds and purples are from oyster lichen, Jell-O and brazilwood. The blues are food coloring, the greens from onion skins overdyed with food coloring, and the browns and tans from onion skins with parmelia lichen. It's very satisfying to use natural dyes.

SOMETHING BEAUTIFUL! I was so pleased with my successful attempt to combine English locker hooking with Portuguese counted cross-stitching that I just had to show off this runner rug. Helping me is Lisa Scharf, a research scientist from Adak who is also a spinner. Incidentally, the photo was taken by Jim Schneeweis, a biologist from the University of Minnesota who was working on the research vessel Tiglax. Lisa and Jim stopped in our harbor to get out of the weather.

COLORS TO DYE FOR. The buttercups will make a bright orange dye. Put 1 pound in a non-reacting pot with enough water to float yarn. Add 2 ounces of wet yarn; simmer 15 minutes. Remove yarn; add pinch of tin crystals dissolved in boiling water. Simmer 20 minutes and cool overnight in dye bath. To get a green dye from geraniums, put 1 pound in an iron pot with water to float 1 ounce of yarn, simmer 1 hour, cool overnight in dye bath, rinse and dry in shade.

The Thousand-Mile Mall

I share your letters with my kids in class. They wonder if you miss going to the mall. Do you crave a Big Mac, pizza or other fast foods? —Danita Shaw, Lesage, West Virginia

WE ADMIRE teachers who enrich their students' knowledge in different ways. Danita is one of the many teachers I've discovered who use *Country* magazine in their classrooms.

"If you wait long enough, the sea will bring you whatever you want," Milt told the boys when we first moved to Chernofski. They soon discovered the 1,200 miles of coastline contained everything a mall did...except a checkout counter.

The reef made a great deli—mussels, sea urchins and pogies were always specialties of the day. Any driftwood log pile was a hardware store when it gave up pieces of shipwrecks.

The toy department provided abundant baseball bats, lost overboard from fishing boats whose crew members used them to break up ice that formed on railings and wheelhouses during winter storms.

The antique section held weathered cedar buoys, glass fishing floats from Japan and Russia, dented canteens from WWII, Russian ax heads and once, a cut glass kerosene lamp.

The post office delivers messages in bottles from as far away as Hawaii.

And anything can float into the gift shop. "It's almost Mom's birthday," I once overheard Chuck tell Randall. "We better hit the beaches."

They returned with big grins and bulging pockets, excited about the Korean beer they had found. I let them try one and they even pretended they

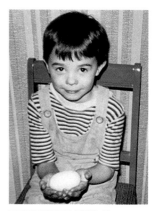

THREE-YOLKER. Even at age 5, Randall preferred treasures not found in stores. For example, he loved to gather eggs, like this one he was sure was a three-yolker. His love of gathering carried over to Unalaska.

WHOSE DEAL? It was a special treat when Grandma Gorley spent Christmas with us in Idaho, as she did in 1978 (right, with Randall and Chuck). Back in the lower 48, the boys learned that playing gin rummy with Grandma Gorley was more fun than going to the mall.

CHOP, CHOP, BOYS. They all pitched in at Grandma's Gorley's, where Randall and Chuck chopped and split firewood one fall (left). They were rewarded when Grandma took them fishing.

BABY AND THE BEAR. Danita Shaw (below left with husband Kem and son Caleb) wanted to know about malls and pizzas. Kem, with the Department of Natural Resources, deals with other subjects (below).

47

liked it. When my birthday arrived, they surprised me with a unique basket-covered jug and a beautiful coral-encrusted shell.

As for pizza, we enjoy it often!

Cora's Easy Pizza

Crust:
   1 tablespoon yeast
   1 tablespoon sugar
   1 teaspoon salt
   1 cup warm water
   1 tablespoon oil
   3 cups flour

Dissolve yeast, sugar and salt in water. Add oil and enough flour to make a soft dough. Knead for 5 minutes. Roll out immediately and place in a round baking pan.

Filling:

Lightly oil unbaked crust; spread with one 16-ounce can of tomato sauce. Sprinkle with a generous pinch of Italian seasonings. Cover with 4 ounces of mozzarella cheese. Arrange a pound of browned sausage, hamburger or pepperoni over cheese. Add one 4-ounce can of sliced olives and one 4-ounce can of button mushrooms. Drain a 16-ounce can of pineapple tidbits and sprinkle over mushrooms. Top with 4 ounces of shredded medium cheddar cheese. Bake 45 minutes in a hot oven, checking frequently and covering with foil if browning too fast. Pour the reserved pineapple juice into a quart of Tang; serve with pizza.

NO SULKING. In Idaho, Chuck liked his pony and sulky better than going to the mall. He could always find something fun to do outdoors. Most of the time, he and he friends hung out together hunting or riding their bikes. Up in Unalaska, Chuck discovered he missed strawberries and bananas more than he missed Big Macs. And he loves Mom's pizza (see the recipe above).

Making a Living

How do you make money to buy those supplies you order every 2 years? —*Matthew Tucker, Oakboro, North Carolina*

THAT'S A GOOD QUESTION, Matthew, one we ask ourselves from time to time.

Wool has always been our "cash crop", but these days, it isn't worth shipping to the lower 48. So we aren't paying for many supplies with our sheep.

PAYDAY FOR RANDALL. One source of income was the pelts from the foxes on the island. Here Randall carried home two pelts from his trapline. He had to use snowshoes on some days and found that skinning the foxes where he trapped them made his load lighter. No, that isn't his long hair you see. Those are the flaps from the beaver hat under his cap.

Still, Milt and I like sheep, and want to keep raising them. We eat and sell their meat. I spin their wool and use it for clothing, rugs and yarn to sell. We have their hides tanned and sell them for rugs in the village 80 miles away. So we feel that our 400 sheep still pay their way.

We raise cattle, but they are hard to market from way out here. They give us meat and sometimes milk. We sell old ones to fishing boats for bait to use in their crab pots. We make jerky.

We trap fox and sell or trade their pelts. That's what Randall has always done for hard cash.

We collect usable fishing gear from the beaches and sell it to the fishermen.

I write articles for magazines.

We don't need large sums of money. Our meat is free. We raise chickens for eggs and meat. We fish for seafood. We eat clams and mussels. We burn wood from the beach and coal from a big pile the military left in 1944. We entertain ourselves by reading and working. There is no place to spend money, so we don't miss having a lot.

CASH ON THE HOOF. The sheep and cattle raised at Chernofski provide food and income. Sheep are sheared (as Chuck is doing above) for wool, and the hides are sold (above right) or turned into items for the house, like the carpeting in the library (right). Those black-and-white hides are tanned by a process that allows them to be tossed into the washer and dryer. Cattle (below) provide food and sometimes milk, as well as income from visiting fishing boats.

BUOYING SPIRITS. After sorting buoys for a while, I took a break (above). I was glad I didn't have to help Randall and Milt gather the buoys they found on the beach. Randall used his rubber dinghy to row ashore and tie a line to the buoys. Milt then pulled them out to his 16-foot boat. One time, the line from Milt's boat and the dinghy was too short, and when it hit the end, Randall took an unwanted bath.

FREE ENTERTAINMENT. The best parts of Unalaska are free, like walking the beach and enjoying the surf, as Randall and I did one day (below). On this day, in July 1983, the breakers appeared taller than me, although I didn't go into the surf to check. Without the man-made "improvements" of civilization, such as billboards and fast-food places, the views are great. That's Umnak Island in the background.

MOBILE MUTTON. Chuck takes another load of one cash crop, mutton, down the shaky dock for shipment to Unalaska Village (above).

FREE-LANCER AT WORK. Some of the income on the ranch comes from my writing (below). Writing is a lot more fun than cleaning the house!

How Do You Catch a Wild Mustang?

Randall takes the cake—he surely keeps you on your toes. Life on the island would have been pretty dull without him. I wonder how he enticed the wild horses to capture them.
—Loraine Lundin, Auberry, California

THE FIRST TIME Randall saw wild horses running free on the west end of the island, he promised himself that someday he'd have one.

From that day on, he started planning. Saving his trapping money for a whole year, he bought a motorbike from the village store, then traded some fox pelts to a boat captain to persuade him to bring it to the ranch.

Randall and Milt discussed endless strategies to catch a wild colt, finally agreeing to try the motorbike, the Ferret and two horses.

On March 3, 1985, during the worst winter in 15 years, Randall, Milt and Rick Nelson, a hired hand, caught a wild colt by chasing a winter-thin band into a gully filled with snow. One 4-month-old got stuck.

With luck and a lot of determination, Randall scrambled into the snowbank and roped the colt. With his own band gone, the colt followed the ranch horses back to headquarters.

Randall named him "Muckle-Dun"

SPOILED CHILD? This mustang colt, "Muckle-Dun", was Randall's first horse and everyone's favorite. Milt enjoyed spoiling the colt with extra oats as much as Randall did. Randall spent every spare minute with his colt.

for his light coloring. Since the colt didn't know what oats were, Randall scoured the frozen hillsides for grass, cutting a feed sack full every day until Muckle-Dun caught onto eating grain. Randall loved that colt and spent every minute he could steal from his classes out in the barn petting and grooming him.

Muckle-Dun became a gentle, willing mount, and Randall rode him over every inch of the ranch. They were inseparable and Randall was heartsick when Muckle-Dun died from a severe wire injury.

Randall caught his next horse, "Montie", by sheer luck. He chased him away from a wild band with his bike and the horse got in with a couple ranch packhorses and followed them home.

After that, he caught six more colts by himself, usually by isolating them from their bands and herding them into the ranch horses, which he brought along for lures.

SAILING MANES. *Tails and manes flew for a time while the mustangs got used to being with the ranch horses. "Rusty", the red mustang (below), would take on any horse, no matter its size. But he turned out to be one of the best horses, strong and smart, gentled by handling and maturity.*

TREATS FOR THE TRIO. "Velvet", "Montie" and "Buck" make sure they don't leave one oat of their winter ration for the birds or sheep. After living on grass in the wild, it took the mustangs a while to learn to eat oats.

RANDALL'S GIFT. We called this mustang filly "Ghost Girl" because of her unusual light coloring and palomino-like mane and tail. Randall caught her and then gave her to me as a gift.

BORN FREE. Mustangs doing what they do best, running wild across the tundra.

GHOST GIRL'S GIRL. Randall got a bonus when "Ghost Girl" gave birth. The foal, which was Ghost Girl's third, was named "Indiana".

INSEPARABLE PAIR. The summer of 1984, when I was sick with cancer, Muckle-Dun was Randall's biggest pleasure. Randall taught the horse to pull in harness, and even used him to drag a skiff, which had washed up on the Pacific side, 5 miles to the ranch. Randall rode Muckle-Dun bareback, sometimes without even a halter. He could also vault onto the horse's back from behind.

Let's Try One More Time

What is your philosophy of life? What kind of characteristics do you have that make you want to live the way you do?
—Colleen Vorisek, Chappaqua, New York

An eighth-grade schoolteacher, Colleen describes herself as spiritual in nature.

She read the first *Country* article about Chernofski to her students because she wanted them to know not everyone in America lived the same way they did.

I think we are spiritual by nature, too. We're not affiliated with any church, but we worship every day and give thanks for being where we are.

Philosophy wasn't a subject I spent much time thinking about when my head was crowded with traffic, mortgages, Cub Scouts and grocery bills.

Until I met Milt, I fought all my battles by withdrawing. Unlike my sons, who saw Chernofski as a great adventure, I saw it as a refuge—from a high-pressure job, from urban living, from raising my kids in an environment where I had no control.

By running away to Alaska, I learned how to stand and fight. It didn't happen all at once, but Milt showed me how without saying a word.

The first Christmas Milt and I spent alone at the ranch called for something different than our usual festivities, which we knew would make us miss the kids that much more.

Since it was a beautiful warm winter day, we motored across the harbor with our wooden dory to beachcomb. We tied the boat to a piling beside a small abandoned military pier and walked for miles in the sunshine.

Being without the boys gave us an unexpected sense of freedom and we didn't even care how late it got. One cove after another beckoned, and when we finally started back, it was late in the afternoon with twilight crowding us.

When we returned to the boat, it was high and dry on the

beach with teasing little waves lapping against its stern.

We pushed and rocked on the bow in hopes it might shift and slide backward into the water, but we didn't waste much energy doing that because both of us knew we didn't have a prayer of pushing that 2,000-pound boat an inch, much less the foot we needed.

"Let's walk to the slaughterhouse," I suggested. "It's only a mile or so and we can build a fire." Dusk had fallen and a little breeze made my damp clothes feel cold.

"Yeah, we might have to," Milt agreed. "But first let's try prying. See if you can find some rocks."

He hurried down the beach and came back with a driftwood pole twice his height, scraped a depression in the gravel under the bow and jammed in the pole. "Wedge a rock behind it," he directed.

When the rock was in place, he leaned all his weight on the pole, but the boat didn't budge. I added my weight, and we balanced on the end of the pole and bounced up and down.

"We're not strong enough," I panted. "It's dark, and I'm cold. I want to go to the slaughterhouse."

"Let's try one more thing." Milt got in the boat and rummaged under the bow while I jogged in place and shivered.

"Glad I had this with me." He climbed out with an armful of rope and dangling pulleys. "You never know when a block and tackle will come in handy." He hooked one end to the stern and dragged the rest under the dock.

"How long is this going to take?" I called after him, hating the petulance in my voice. I was freezing. All the fingers on my missing right hand felt like they were doubled up and throbbing inside my fiberglass arm as they always did when I got cold.

"Not long," he yelled over his shoulder. "Get the flashlight and see what the tide is doing."

I pointed the beam toward the stern. "Oh, no," I cried. "It's still going out."

Where an hour before small waves were lapping at the boat bottom, now wet gravel stretched for 8 inches. "We'll never get off here till the tide comes in." I stamped my frozen feet. "Please, can't we stay in the slaughterhouse and come back in the morning?"

"I wish we could." I heard the limping scrunch of his boots on the gravel. He took the flashlight and waved it along the water's edge. "I think it's starting in," he said, then tilted the light at my face. "You're cold. Why don't you walk to the slaughterhouse and get a fire started."

"All by myself?" I quavered.

He flashed the light along the water once again, "I'll come start the fire." He pocketed the light and took my hand, urging me up the beach toward the grass.

IMMOVABLE OBJECT. When the water went out from under this 2,000-pound dory, it took a lot of positive thinking, and elbow grease, to get it afloat again. But the experience taught a lesson—never give up, and carry a tide chart.

"But you'll come back, won't you?" I yelled. "It's the middle of the night, but I know you. You'll work on this miserable boat until you get it off even if it takes till tomorrow." I glared at him. "Well, I'm not leaving without you," I shouted. "And if I freeze to death, it will be your fault."

"The wind has changed. We'll lose the boat if it really starts blowing in here," he said quietly. "I want to try the block and tackle; if it doesn't work, then we'll go."

I wanted to hit him. I felt the wind and heard its whistle across the water, and the more I knew he was right, the more I wanted to hit him, pound some sense into him, get through to him that it wasn't a crime to give into tiredness and insurmountable odds. But he was gone, crawling along the face of the dilapidated pier with his ropes and pulleys.

Angry as I was, I still got at the water's edge and aimed the light toward the farthest piling. He was hanging head down off the dock face getting his tackle rope into place around the piling.

"Okay," he gasped as he rushed past me with the rope braced around his waist. "Get on that pry pole and wiggle the bow." I heard him groan with exertion as he pulled.

I dropped the light and leaned on the pry pole without hope, going through the motions, wanting only to be someplace else, wanting to scream "I told you so!" as all our efforts failed to move the squat wooden monster that was stuck to the beach like a leech.

"Nope, I'm not strong enough to pull the blocks together," Milt rasped finally, throwing down the rope.

"Can we go now?" I retrieved the light and flicked it on. His face looked so worried and bleak in the yellow light, with the ever-increasing wind blowing his beard and hair into a mad tangle, that I wished for his sake there really was something we could do.

"In a minute," he said. Limping back to the boat, he dragged out a cable with a pulley and ratchet on it. "I'll give this come-along one try, then we'll go." Within seconds, he had one end of it anchored to a piling farther along the beach and the other tied to the rope he had been pulling on.

"Okay." He strained against the ratchet that moved the cable a fraction of an inch at a time. "Pry on the bow with the bar," he shouted over the wind.

I pushed and he worked the lever for what seemed like hours. Actually it was hours, at least 1, before we felt the boat move even an inch, and 3 before it came off the beach.

When the boat slid into the water with the wind slapping spray into our faces, we were both so exhausted we didn't even feel it. But I wasn't cold any longer.

Back home, with the chores done and the warm fire I had longed for earlier finally a reality, we ate our Christmas dinner of peanut butter and jelly sandwiches at midnight and savored every bite.

Afterward, with our feet stuck in the oven and steaming mugs of tea in our hands, we discussed our adventure.

"You know, Milt," I began thoughtfully, "you can do anything you set your mind to. Nothing is impossible for you. That taught me a good lesson about myself tonight."

"Taught me a good lesson, too," he grumbled. "After this, I won't forget to check the danged tide book before I leave the house."

WONDERFUL WARMTH. There's nothing like 4 hours of fighting a beached dory to make a good wood fire feel welcome. Bring on the hot tea and peanut butter and jelly sandwiches.

Heard from Another Country

I am very excited about your life. I think it is very difficult but beautiful. I know the television show "Northern Exposure" is not very realistic, but it shows life there that way. People are friendly and help each other in hard times. They simply live. Do you visit other parts of your country, and do people visit you sometimes?   *—Alicja Roston, Koblyka, Poland*

WE'VE never seen *Northern Exposure* but are happy that it shows Alaska as a place where people are friendly and like to help each other.

We welcome everyone who comes into the harbor. Whether from near or far, visitors who get as far beyond the sidewalks as Chernofski Sheep Ranch have a special aura of adventure about them. They make world geography come to life in a way classroom lectures never can.

Many leave behind a part of themselves in their stories and

WORLD TRAVELERS. Fog surrounds Bill and Mary Black of Seattle, Washington as they row past our anchored skiff to their sailboat, Foreign Affair, in the background. I think this photo is a fitting tribute to Bill and Mary, as they had just completed a 10-year-long world tour that started right here in Chernofski Harbor.

the help they gave us. We glimpse their world through their photographs and sometimes a message under their name in our guest book, like these...

John Wilmer, Iceland: "Thanks for the lamb head."

Joyce Van Vleet, California: "A nice place to spend a honeymoon."

Hal Slovers, fishing vessel *Lyada*: "Thanks for letting me ride your horses. What a thrill."

John Gore-Grimes, Dublin, Ireland: "As we say in Ireland,

YAKKING WITH KAYAKERS. After watching the 1978 British kayak expedition and the 1986 German kayak expedition land in the surf on Chernofski's beaches, we talked to leaders Derek Hutchinson of England and Arrved Fuchs of Germany. Milt decided that he was going to stick with his reliable and stable dory.

'Gan eiri an bothair leit.' 'May the road rise up with you.'"

Mark Connor, Michigan: "Arrived on foot with Chuck from Dutch Harbor...12 days."

Josh Forgves, Alaska: "Stepped back 50 years, and caught up."

Arrved Fuchs and the crew of *Dagmar Aaen*: "On our way to the Siberian Arctic. Thanks for the hospitality."

Frances Tolbert, Alaska: "What a lovely, lovely spot."

Diana Brown, Colorado: "You are living the life most people only dream of."

Lee Hudson, Canada: "Great place. Feels like home."

HEAT AND EAT. No matter where our visitors come from, there's something for everyone at Chernofski. Jonathan Larrivee and Jill Mitchell of New Zealand (above) found warmth by the kitchen stove, while Canadians Henry McCarty, Bruce Hubbard, Pat Harvie and Patty Hubbard (at left, left to right) gathered around for an impromptu, if chilly, cookout.

Harold and Hedel Voss, sailors from West Germany: "Thank you very much for your hospitality."

Lynne Johnson, Washington State: "Wonderfully peaceful atmosphere. God did good."

When Alaska Was Still a Territory—Guest Book Quotes 1948-1959

Slim Stabenauc: "Greetings from a sourdough."

USNS T-AKL 33 Second officer Ruders Riolns: "Thank you so much for your hospitality."

USNS T-AKL 33 Jess C. Edwards, Master: "Biscuits like Mother tried to make."

USAF Nigle Captain Roy N. Hough, Seattle, Washington: "Chernofski, the pearl of the Aleutians."

NO PROBLEM. Getting off Chernofski's beach in the surf was child's play for Willy Kerr, skipper of the 32-foot yacht Assent, and a sheep farmer from Somerset, England. Along with writer John Gore-Grimes and Tom Lawlor of Dublin, Ireland, Willy sailed across the Bering Sea to Russia and back.

TOO MANY COOKS? Luckily, the kitchen at Chernofski is big enough for a friendly competition. Because when representatives of such diverse cuisines as Louisiana, New Mexico and Canada gathered around my Alaskan cookstove, a cook-off was inevitable. The contestants are, from left to right, Nancy Eyl, Louisiana; Chris Jobe, Alberta; Francesca Cordova, New Mexico; Cora; and Dawnelle Frohler and Marie Rawe, both also from Alberta. Now you're probably wondering who the winners were. Well, those who ate the entries, of course.

GOOD-BYE, ALASKA. Fifteen-year-old Randall got off his motorcycle long enough to say good-bye to a group of archaeologists who stayed in our bunkhouse for a week while they surveyed historic landmarks for the Alaska Native Association.

POLAR EXPEDITION. Arrved Fuchs and crew sailed into Chernofski Harbor again in 1994 aboard the Dagmar Aaen (above) on their way over the North Pole. They were trying to sail to Hamburg, Germany by way of the Siberian Arctic.

MORE SAILORS. Hedel and Harold Voss from Germany (left) took a break from their yacht, Moritz B, and their world cruise to come ashore and visit with us at Chernofski.

BUSY PLACE. When a Grumman Goose landed to load a group of departing Canadian guests at the same time as seismologists from Stanford University arrived, the beach at Chernofski looked like Grand Central Station.

BIG WATER, LITTLE BOAT. Not everyone sails into Chernofski Harbor in a yacht. This 8-foot homemade sailboat and its 10-year-old skipper were lowered off a fishing boat by a proud grandfather, who then helped navigate across the bay for a visit at the ranch.

WORKING VACATION. Milt often takes guests for a jaunt across the tundra. This usually starts off as a joyride. But I know Milt, and I bet that most of the time, he had them round up some cattle or sheep.

How About a Job?

You live the best life-style—no people, no cars, how wonderful. My town has only 54 people, but that's still way too many for me.

My mom is as bad, or maybe even worse, at worrying about teenagers than you seemed to be in your book. My brother and I drive our mom nutty. I'm only 16, so I'm still high on adventure, like cliff climbing. That's my mother's least favorite activity.

I don't want to be nosy, but have you ever considered hiring teenage kids? Some kids would give their eyeteeth to live there and work. —Kami Good, Murphy, Idaho

THE FIRST CHARACTERISTIC about Milt that made me notice him as a person, rather than as just an employer, was his kindness to my sons. He was genuinely interested in them as individuals. As I got to know Milt, I discovered that besides raising two sons of his own, he had given summer jobs to kids from the surrounding villages as long as he had been here.

In 1982, *National Geographic* sent photographer Steve Wilson to Unalaska on assignment for an article about the Aleutian Islands. When he visited our ranch, he told Milt that many of the people he had interviewed said the high point in their life was the summer they spent working at Chernofski.

SOCK HOP. When "Jazzy Baby", a bum lamb, bleated for his bottle, 6-year-old Reece Hubbard didn't even take time to put on his shoes. Hey, are those socks wool?

GIFT HORSE. Summer employee Crystal Anderson spent every minute she could spare from her kitchen duties with "Pixie", the Morgan filly Milt gave her.

GET ALONG, OLD DOGIE. Ten-year-old Jesse Hubbard joined the round-up and hazed along a bull that was about the same age as he was.

PRETTY CORNY. Erin Dickson (below) ground some corn for the chickens.

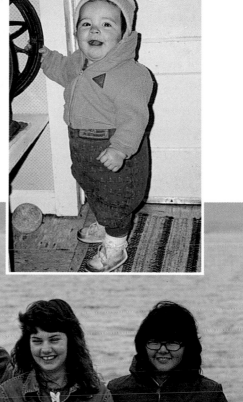

FUZZY PAIR. Taylor and "Jasper" (the lamb above) kept an eye on each other.

WHO'S STEERING? Summer employees Nena Yatchmenoff (left) and Lillian Bereskin (right) rode while visitor Lisa Allbee took the wheel. Milt, who was giving a ride to the three girls from Unalaska Village, became a backseat driver for a while.

HOME ON THE RANGE. When Milt's youngest son, Val, grew up on the ranch, the winters were quiet and filled with studies. But when summer came, things got exciting, and Val was able to meet kids from up and down the Aleutian Islands when they came to the ranch to put in a season of work for Milt.

WHAT A MESS! Although summers were busy, with lots of work for everyone, Milt gave the kids time to enjoy themselves. Nicky Dushkin (left), from Nikolski, Alaska, and Tommy Horn, from Umnak, Alaska, relaxed between such jobs as wrangling sheep and stomping wool by catching this string of Dolly Varden trout.

CATTLE CALL. A young crew helps Milt (right, in red cap) count cattle coming down the chute.

POOPED PUP. We don't hire kids anymore. But we do invite working guests, and the biggest problem is getting them to stop at quitting time—like Bryce Hubbard, who tired himself out feeding bum calves (below), then needed a snooze in the kitchen rocker before supper (right).

Kids Want to Know...

What is Alaska really like?   —*Dionna Steele*
Twentynine Palms, California

FIRST OF ALL, Alaska is a big state. If you laid it over the continental United States, it would stretch from New York to Texas. And all of it is different.

Alaska has a small population, just over half a million people. Our capital city is Juneau (it's the only state capital not accessible by road). Our biggest city is Anchorage, where half the population of the state lives.

Fairbanks is up north and much colder than the Aleutian Islands. They have shorter winter days and longer summer days. They see the northern lights in winter. They can grow huge cabbages and strawberries and other vegetables because of the long hours of sunshine. The main branch of the University of Alaska is there.

The northernmost town in Alaska is Barrow. It is mostly a native town. Eskimos still kill whales for food. They have polar bears, but the people do not live in igloos. The people are very proud of their heritage and ancestry.

There aren't many people in the Aleutian Islands, only a few villages and one town of any size, Unalaska-Dutch Harbor. It is one of the biggest fishing ports in the world. Fishing is the main industry for the islands. There is also a military installation on Adak, an island farther west. Nobody can go there without clearance.

When I taught my sons Alaskan geography, I divided Alaska into six parts:

First is the panhandle, where the capital is. It is wet and rainy, with over 200 inches of rain falling annually in some places.

Then there's the Cook Inlet area, which includes Anchorage, the Kenai Peninsula and the Matanuska Valley. This portion of the state holds over half the population.

Next is the interior, where it's dry and cold and very sparsely populated.

The northern part above the Arctic Circle is covered with permafrost and inhabited by hardy Eskimos.

Further west is the coastal region that includes Nome, where gold was discovered at the turn of the century. Reindeer and musk-oxen live there.

Finally the Aleutian Islands are damp, windswept and hidden from the outside world with fog. Aleuts live here and are very proud of their ancient heritage.

When the Russians came, they brought new customs and beliefs, which the Aleuts assimilated into their own culture. They cherish the Russian Orthodox church on Unalaska Island. It is the oldest church building in Alaska, rebuilt around 1826.

Here on our ranch it's just us and a lot of sheep, cattle and horses. We love it that way.

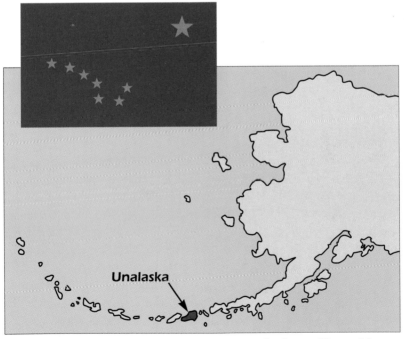

ALASKA IS BIG! The map of Alaska, if laid over the lower 48, would stretch from New York to Texas. The state flag (inset) depicts the Big Dipper and the North Star.

Chickens in the Wind

I read your book twice and then my husband read it. We agreed your home island was interesting but a good place to be far away from. That wind! How do the chickens and other small animals stay put?   *—Jeanne Wachter, Hubbard, Nebraska*

IT SEEMS ODD, but the smaller the animal, the better chance it has of staying put in the wind—especially if they crouch low to the ground.

I've seen horses stagger and dance sideways while trying to run to the grain feeder in a windstorm. Our chickens and rabbits, meanwhile, just hunker down and keep on eating. If the storm has rain or snow, the small animals will go back into their houses or get under them.

Even the large animals find something, like a hill or building, to hide behind. Our horses, especially, seem to congregate behind the picket gate that leads out of the yard. I can't imagine why—it offers almost no protection, although they can see the grain feeder from there.

The only time I saw an animal actually in danger of becoming airborne was right after Milt and I were married. We had a ewe and lamb in the yard because the ewe was a real grandmother and I wanted to keep an eye on the baby.

I put a plastic coat on the lamb to protect him from the April storms. The first time the wind came up and that lamb turned his little backside to it, a gust went under the plastic. He took about three giant leaps trying to keep up with his coat, then took off like a hang glider until he fetched up against the fence, where he immediately hid in the tall grass.

We decided he knew more about keeping warm than we did, so we took the coat off and let him take care of himself.

GROUND-POUNDERS. Chickens, built low to the ground, just hunker down and keep on pecking when the wind blows. The bigger animals have problems.

By Plane, by Boat, by Foot

I'm interested in your area, because from October 1943 through March 1945, I was a sailor stationed at the naval base in Dutch Harbor. I've been trying to pinpoint your ranch location. Where the confusion enters is with your book saying that the nearest town is 110 miles away. I thought this might be a typo since Unalaska Island is only about 75 miles from east to west.
—Kenneth Robb, New Harmony, Indiana

THE DISTANCE between Unalaska Village and Chernofski Sheep Ranch depends on the method of travel and the weather.

On a clear windless day, a plane can fly up Captain's Bay, follow Shaishnikof River, cross the Shaler Mountains and fly down the backbone of the island to the ranch for a distance of about 65 miles.

But if the pilot is beset by fog and wind, and has to crawl along the coastline around Kovrizhka and follow the shore all

HOW FAR IS IT? Distances are relative on Unalaska Island. The distance between Unalaska Village and the ranch depends on how you travel. But even by boat, the distance can go from 70 to 100 miles, if you have to hug the coastline and dash into hiding when the weather gets bad. Flying can also mean taking detours if the pilot faces wind and fog. Walking involves crossing all kinds of different terrain, including mountains and cliffs. What might be 65 miles by air, can easily be 110 on the ground, considering all the ups and downs.

the way to Chernofski Harbor, it is closer to 90 miles.

The weather plays havoc with boat travel. The 70-mile trip can easily become 100 if you travel in an 18-foot skiff, as Chuck and Randall do. Because their boats are small and open, they both hug the coastline and dash into hiding the moment the weather changes.

When traveling on foot from Unalaska Village to Chernofski Sheep Ranch, the weather isn't as important as the landscape. When terrain includes tundra, bogs, glaciers, the Shaler Mountains, cliffs, hills and alpine meadows, some of those miles can seem very long. We'd guess 110 miles is a conservative estimate when all the ups and downs are considered.

THE EASY WAY. Flying overland down the "backbone" of the island (above) is quick, short and scenic. But it's only possible on clear, windless days, like this one. It also lets you see the rugged country Chuck hiked through from the village to the ranch.

ROCK AND A HARD PLACE. On his hike from Unalaska Village to the ranch, Chuck discovered there were no trails, and shortcuts were few. But Chuck couldn't afford the price of a charter, so he hiked. This rock (left) rose 25 feet out of the water and seemed pretty big as Chuck inched his way across it. But he enjoyed himself enough that he repeated the trip 3 years later, becoming the first man in local history, out of four who made the hike, to do it twice. The first trip took Chuck 13 days, but the second took only 8. Obviously, it pays to know the territory.

Milt's Story in His Own Words

Thank you, thank you, thank you. My daughter, Sandy, bought your book, and words can't express how much I enjoyed reading it. It's a love story besides being an adventure. Thank Milt for keeping the fires going for you to write the book. I'd be interested to hear the story of how Milt arrived at the ranch in 1948.
—Maxine Eads, Lathrop, Missouri

"THE SUMMER I turned 21, during the early 1940s, I was in Idaho herding sheep. Hiking around one day, I came across a place where some sheep herders had camped. I found a newspaper there, so I sat down and began reading the paper to catch up on news from the war.

"I came across an article written by Mrs. Ruth Catron. She was describing this place called Chernofski, where they were taking care of sheep that belonged to Oregon Worsted Woolen Mill, an affiliate of Pendleton Wool.

"She was looking for someone to take back with her to learn the ropes, so to speak, and take over. She felt she and her husband were at the age when they should get out of the ranching game.

MILT'S MOM. Milt came from pioneer stock. In 1917, Paul Holmes took his bride, Ruth (right, in 1914), packed all their possessions into a Studebaker wagon pulled by a pair of good mules and moved to a homestead near Midvale, Idaho, in the shadow of Hitt Mountain, on a little creek called Surdam.

NOWHERE...10 MILES. Back in the hills, 10 miles from nowhere, Milt's folks quickly built a house and barn. Like most homesteads, the barn was bigger and built much better than the house. After all, the barn protected the livestock and feed, the key to existence—and survival—for pioneers in those early years.

"I had always wanted to go to Alaska, and I already had an uncle there. I had heard some pretty exciting tales about the country.

"There was no way I could apply for the job, as I was tied down with herding our band of sheep and being my own camp tender as well as tending camp for another band while we were in the mountains.

"But it really piqued my interest, so I cut out the article and put it in my billfold, where it stayed until after the war ended and my brothers and sisters were civilians again.

"Then one fall, after we came in from the mountains and put the sheep in pasture, I met a girl from Howe, Idaho, where the people lived who were working on the Chernofski Sheep Ranch.

"Her folks knew people who knew the Catrons, and it turned out they were still looking for someone to come and take over. Since I was the only one who had applied for the job in all those years, I was hired."

BLOOMS IN THE WILDERNESS. Homesteading was hard work, and pretty much a no-frills affair. But by the time Ruth and Paul were expecting their third child in 1921, they had cleared and cultivated most of the land and lived, for the most part, on what the homestead provided. Some of those provisions came from the garden Ruth and daughters Leanor and Peggy (above) were so proud of.

WELCOME, MILT. On August 10, 1921, Milt and his twin sister, Mildred, were born...at home, of course. That's Milt on the left (above) being held by Mom. There was no way to get to a doctor out there, 10 miles into the hills, with the only transportation by team and wagon. So Ruth's brother took a fast horse to get the doctor. The doctor missed Mildred's birth because three other babies were being born around Midvale that day. Besides that, the doctor was driving a Model T Ford that had to be pulled up Lightning Point Hill by an obliging wood-hauler and his team of horses. But the doctor got there in time for Milt's birth, whose arrival was a real surprise, as they were not expecting twins. By the time they were 3 months old, the tiny twins could be taken outside for a photograph on their mother's lap, along with Leanor and Peggy.

WHAT A HAT! By 1925, at 4 years old, Milt was already stepping into his role as eldest son by wearing his father's hat (above). Milt never lacked for playmates, growing up on the homestead. He had three sisters and a baby brother. In fact, Milt was 5 years old before he met another child that wasn't a member of his own family.

OFF TO SCHOOL. In 1926, when Milt was 5, the family moved to Midvale so the kids could go to school instead of being home-taught. Milt's father got a job tending the community's sheep flock. But every summer, all five children went back to their home in the mountains, with sister Leanor in charge, for 3 months of freedom and adventure. It would not be long before Milt would follow in his father's bootsteps and learn to love the life of a sheep man.

BIBLICAL PROFESSION. Milt and his father trailing sheep (left) the summer after a Christmas experience that convinced Milt he wanted to be a sheep man. I'll let him tell it. "I knew I wanted to be a sheep man during one Christmas vacation when I spent 10 days helping my dad trail sheep to their feed yards in the lower country. On Christmas Eve, we got permission from a rancher, who had a place out against the foothills, to put our sheep in his field for the night. The rancher, who was named Chadwick, came out to our camp that night for a visit. He brought along his son, who was about 4 or 5. On Christmas morning, bright and early, Mr. Chadwick came back out to invite us into the house for breakfast because his son was so excited about us being there. 'It's just like in the Bible, Daddy,' the little fellow had told his folks. 'And the shepherds waited in the fields with their flocks.' Later in the day, when we let the sheep stop to eat and rest, I laid down in the warm winter sun and thought about what the little boy had said. I knew then that tending sheep was what I wanted to do with my life."

TEEN TENDER. With his horse, dogs and camp tent, Milt looked older than his 15 years when he started his career tending sheep. "I guess being born and raised in the mountains made me always feel more comfortable and at ease when I was out in the hills," Milt says. "So herding sheep came naturally to me. When Dad wanted me to come help with the sheep, I was more than happy to quit school in my sophomore year. I never got around to going back."

TOO TAME. Although most young men would think it high adventure to live the way Milt did when he was 21 (left), Milt wanted more room than Idaho's hills offered, and more adventure than the sheep, packhorses and occasional marauding bear gave him. One day he found an old newspaper and read about the adventures of herding sheep in the Aleutian Islands of Alaska. There was a job there for someone with enough skill and gumption. Milt tucked the article in his wallet and went back to work tending sheep in Idaho. But years later, after the war was over, Milt found out the job was still open, and he was on his way to Chernofski.

BVD BROTHER. Tending sheep became more fun when Milt's younger brother, Tom, came to camp with his bear rifle (left), to say nothing of those long johns and a balky burro (above).

HOME AND AWAY. When Pearl Harbor was attacked and war declared, Milt (above left) had been tending Midvale's community flock with his father for 6 years. He tried three times to enlist, but each time, the local draft board turned him down. They said it took 15 sheep to outfit one soldier, and Milt's job was indispensable. He was to stay where he was. So Milt had to watch sisters Mildred and Peggy and brother Tom (above right) march off to danger and adventure, while he curbed his restlessness and returned to the sheep and the hills. But when the war was over, and Tom, Peggy and Mildred were home safely, it was Milt's turn for adventure. He contacted the people who ran the Chernofski Sheep Ranch, and before long, he was the one leaving home.

NEW HOME.
"Stinker" the sheep-dog checks out his new home the morning after he and Milt arrived at the Chernofski Sheep Ranch. They had traveled for a week by car, train, plane, Army barge and, finally, row-boat. They got to the ranch at night,

where a solitary kerosene lamp in the window welcomed them with a tiny flicker in a very vast darkness.

ALL ABOARD FOR ALASKA. Milt's great adventure was about to begin. It was November 28, 1947, and he was 27. He and "Stinker" were about to board this airplane for Alaska. After the war, a lot of pilots went into the flying business in a small way. So small, in fact, that the stewardess, when there was one, was usually the pilot's girlfriend. And all she had to offer was a blanket and a cup of coffee to ward off hypothermia in the unheated plane. But there was no stewardess on Milt's plane, so he stayed busy trying to keep from freezing to death. In a way, that was good. This was Milt's first flight, and he was too cold to worry about the three harrowing take-off attempts from Seattle, and the emergency night landing on the unlighted runway at Annette Island in Alaska. When Milt transferred to a smaller plane, after a frigid night in the one-room terminal on Annette Is-

land, he again found no stewardess, blankets or hot coffee. Flying from the appropriately named Cold Island to Dutch Harbor, Milt huddled inside his lightweight jacket, while Stinker shivered in the seat next to him. When the pilot came back to check on the passengers, he saw their obvious discomfort and said, "I wouldn't let a dog freeze on a day like this." He then took off his fur parka...and draped it over Stinker.

87

GONE, BUT NOT FORGOTTEN. In 1983, Milt visited the old homestead site on Hitt Mountain in Idaho, where his parents had settled in 1917. The buildings were gone, and all that remained was the lilac bush his mother had planted by the front door.

Hank the Cow Dog
(And Various Other Pets)

Do you have any house pets?

—Dorothy Melcher
Murdo, South Dakota

I DON'T KNOW what qualifies an animal as a house pet. We've had every type of creature we raise in the house except a horse, and that's only because we haven't had any baby horses sick enough to need that kitchen oven-door treatment.

Like today. I have a baby bunny in a box beside the stove because he's too adventuresome for his own good and I'm afraid a fox or Randall's cat will get him before he gets big enough to defend himself.

Despite Milt's pointed reminders that we already have enough pets, this bunny has graduated to having a name, "Snowball". That's a sure guarantee he has achieved pet status, even though he will return to the rabbit house when he's bigger.

HEY, LET'S EAT! "Hank" the cow dog tells us when it's time for supper. Hank is Milt's special pet and constant companion, and the only animal allowed to stay on the porch. It's a good thing Milt likes Hank as much as he does, because as a sheepdog, Hank is a total washout. You'd think that any dog that can race up the barn roof after a Frisbee, pick up his food dish and drop it on the floor to tell us he's hungry and catch a bouncing rubber ball in his teeth, could round up sheep. It's not that he's lazy or dumb. All you have to do is say, "Go git 'em", and Hank is away in a flash, even if the sheep are just specks on the skyline. The trouble is, he never brings them back. In fact, Hank does such a good job of chasing the sheep clear out of the country that I lock him in the barn whenever I go out to gather sheep.

BYE-BYE, BRO'. I gave Hank's brothers and sisters a farewell meal after Milt decided to send them to the village on the first plane that arrived after their birth. Milt knew I'd get so attached to them that I'd want to keep all nine.

COMFORTABLE COMPANIONS. "Dusty" and "Puck", our two Border collies, are more like pets than working dogs. They only help because they like us so much. But they make unobtrusive companions when I take a hike to the creek, as I did on this day.

ON THE PROWL. "Blue", Randall's cat, here doing a little scouting at the dock, usually prowls the barnyard, checking out every manger for unsuspecting birds feeding on the grain scattered by the horses. Bunnies also have to watch out for big Blue.

CANINE SOCIAL SECURITY. "Tippy", our best cow dog, lived to be 21. He was a pensioner for many years. All our animals live long lives because they don't catch any diseases and, of course, they never get run over by cars.

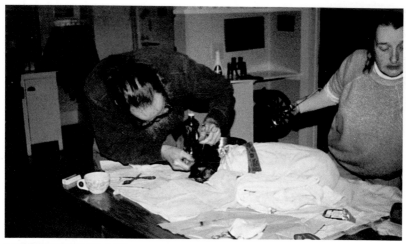

KITCHEN-TABLE VETS. Sometimes accidents do happen to our pets, and we have to take care of them if we can. More than once, our kitchen table has become an "operating table". In 1990, my terrier, "Lilli Belle", needed attention, and Milt took care of her. Although she's now 14, nearly blind and quite deaf, Lilli Belle still enjoys life. She can even feel my footsteps on our wooden walk and jumps up and runs to me. It's a comfort to know that nothing can happen to her here at the ranch. The same could not be said for a blind dog in "civilization".

PILLOW PAL. This wasn't the first time the antique iron bed in the guest room became a luxurious doghouse. Lee Hudson of Canada couldn't resist sneaking a Border collie pup into bed with her to share a nap. Looks like the book the two were reading must have been exciting.

GULLY, THEY'RE CUTE. These baby gulls were rescued by Milt's youngest son, Val. They made great pets for a boy who grew up a long way from a pet store. After Val freed the birds, they'd come back for handouts and get so full they couldn't fly.

CHUCK'S PUP. Chuck's one attempt at raising a puppy was with "Sweetie-Pie", a malamute mix he picked up in the village. Sweetie-Pie settled right into ranch dog life during the 3 months Chuck was here. In fact, Sweetie-Pie considered a spot behind the stove his home. In the spring, when it was time for Chuck to fly out and go back to the village, he headed down the wooden walk with Sweetie-Pie trotting behind him. After our usual flurry of good-byes, Milt and I returned to the house...and found Sweetie-Pie curled up in his usual place, behind the stove.

BUNNY ROOM AND BOARD. These Angora rabbits paid their way by providing me with lots of fuzz for my spinning wheel.

BORN TO RIDE. Val and Mary Dushkin, the foreman's niece, grew up with horses as their best friends and got to know them well. When the horses got big enough to ride, all the kids had to do was hop on their backs. One of these colts grew up to be "Stormy", the Morgan mustang I rode for the first 10 years I lived here.

SAVED BY A BELLE. In 1966, Mary rescued this lamb from a huge flock.

DARING DORY DOG. "Dusty" was a familiar figurehead on the dory when we took trips across the harbor. After a couple of cold baths, and some rough pikepole rescues, he learned to roll with the motion of the waves and stayed high and dry.

PRETTY PLACID PORKERS. These grass-fed pigs made better playmates than bacon. They were gentle enough for Val and Mary to be able to herd them around with sticks. In the winter, though, grass is in short supply.

STOVE-SIDE STUFFERS. Val makes their day as he feeds a couple of piglets. These pampered porkers started their lives beside the kitchen stove, while most pigs end their days on the stove.

A Sequel to 'The Three Little Pigs'
by
Milt Holmes

ALMOST EVERYONE who visits Chernofski Sheep Ranch asks if we have tried raising hogs.

Yes, we did try. We shipped a sow up from Seattle on the mail boat, then borrowed a boar from a man in Unalaska Village who was trying to raise pigs, too.

We all waited. At last, the big day (I should say night) arrived. Our sow, who by this time had become quite a pet, presented us with 10 piglets—and the major problem of no milk. We read all the data we had on pigs and discovered that she was too fat, but she would most likely come to her milk within a few days.

In the meantime, it was a case of resorting to the bottle. I can tell you it didn't take those little pigs long to learn.

Of course, they had to be in a box in the house as they were on a 3-hour schedule. Soon each had a name and they could tell, within a few minutes, when 3 hours were up.

If someone wasn't up and stirring, they would set up the worst squealing you can imagine. They'd keep it up for about 30 seconds, then stop as if on cue and listen. If they didn't hear any feet hitting the floor, especially in the middle of the night, they would start singing again.

As soon as they heard someone talking, they would stop screaming and just grunt, gurgle and make hungry noises until they got their bottles.

When the sow came to her milk, we put the piglets back on her. But by then, it was too late…they were pets.

As time went on, the piglets grew up and had babies, and we were soon overrun with pigs. When they were little and cute, we couldn't make ourselves butcher them, and an old grass-fed pig is very tough and doesn't even taste like pork.

So we hauled them across the harbor in our boat and set them free. They thrived in the summer. In the winter, I'd go feed them corn occasionally, until they associated the sound of my outboard engine with food.

Once a boat came in, and the pigs heard it. The fisherman was trying to get tied up to the dock when this herd of huge pigs came thundering down the runway. He jumped back on his boat and anchored way out in the middle of the bay.

Lucky for him, the pigs didn't know how to swim. However, they did make efficient miniature bulldozers. With their snouts, they rooted up large sections of tundra looking for roots. The Bureau of Land Management didn't like that and suggested we go out of the pig business.

Since the folks who raised pigs in Unalaska stopped even before we did, we buy our ham and bacon now or go without.

No Sequel to 'The Three Billy Goats Gruff'

What about goats? Have you ever tried to raise them at Chernofski? —*Melissa Tordson, Lakefield, Minnesota*

I'VE OFTEN WONDERED how goats would do here. In 1983, two fellows in Unalaska Village shipped some in for pets and kept them for several years.

They seemed to forage well enough for themselves, but they got so wild and ornery, no one could go out to Morris Cove, where they were kept, without being attacked by the billy who had sharp pointed horns. I don't know what the eventual fate of those animals was, but they are no longer there.

When I was growing up in northern Idaho, my folks had a goat dairy. I hated goats then, having to get up practically in the middle of the night to help get them all milked before going to school. Now that "Tulip", our milk cow, ran off, I wouldn't mind having some for milk again. Goats are easier to milk than a cow and small enough for me to handle.

THREE KIDS WITH TWO KIDS. I grew up with goats and hated them then, as I had to get up practically in the middle of the night to milk them. This rare photo from my childhood in Idaho shows me (on the right), my sister Alice beside me and baby sister Kathy behind us. The goats foraged for their own food in the scrubby hillsides. They provided us with meat and, of course, the milk I had to help pull out of them before I went to school each morning. I miss the milk, but not the milking.

MOHAIR TO SPARE. Virginia Collar of Michigan sent this snapshot of her twin Angora goats to compare with our Columbia sheep. The Angoras' fleece is called mohair. Virginia sent along a sample, and I found it a pleasure to spin. It's very different from wool. It has a loose crimp, silky texture and bright luster.

The Land of the Midnight Sun

Do you have the long days of Alaska?   *—Dorothy Melcher*
Murdo, South Dakota

FOR a special Christmas gift, we look forward to December 21 and the promise it brings...3 extra minutes of daylight.

When Chuck was growing up, he'd stand at the window with his hands cupped to the glass even on the gloomiest days and peer into the storms, then say with a big grin on his face, "I can stand anything as long as I know the days are getting longer."

At 53:15° north latitude, we are far enough south to get about 7 hours of light during our short winter days.

The sun rises far to the southeast and scoots around the rim of our southern sky so its rays reach us at an angle, which decreases their warmth.

Storm clouds cover the sky much of the winter, so we spend 8 weeks in muted twilight. Those days are just right for spinning, reading and catalog-shopping, but not as convenient for riding across the island on horseback or venturing out into the water in a small open boat.

So we use every minute of our 18-hour summer days, when the light is still good at 1 a.m. We prepare for winter by hauling coal, gathering wood, shearing and shifting sheep from pasture to pasture and spreading cattle around in the many bays.

SUMMER AND WINTER. High noon in the summer (top right) means sunshine for 18 hours and a view all the way to Mount Tulik, an active volcano on our neighboring island, Umnak. High noon in the winter (right) means twilight-like days, with 7 hours of daylight and only a glimmer of light far to the south.

WINTER TWILIGHT. For about 8 weeks in the winter, we spend our days in muted twilight. But that gives me time for my spinning, and we can catch up on our reading and, of course, catalog-shopping. It's not as much fun when we have to go out for the various chores. But summer always comes, and there'll be days filled with sunshine and time to beachcomb for some more glass floats to catch the light (left).

A Potentially Deadly Gift

You have my admiration to live so remote. I couldn't do it. I've gotten too modern. Since you are remote from the public, do you get fewer colds and flu, etc.? —Dorothy Melcher
Murdo, South Dakota

WE NEVER get colds or flu unless a visitor brings us a bug. We have no resistance because we are not exposed to the viruses and bacteria that most people are. They are so immune, they don't even realize they are bringing us a potential killer.

When that happens, we get seriously ill. Milt, especially, is susceptible because he hasn't been around germs much in the last 50 years. He also has closer contact with passersby, shakes hands with pilots and captains and in general is more visible to outsiders than I am in the kitchen.

So, while I can't remember the last time I was sick with a cold, Milt's last siege is still a vivid memory.

Tom Madsen, our village bush pilot friend, stopped to pick up a load of mutton. He had several passengers on board and introduced them all to Milt when they got off the plane to stretch their legs as the mutton was being loaded.

One fellow in particular noticed that Milt's gloves were full of holes and insisted that he take his new ones, so Milt traded gloves and loaded the rest of the meat.

By that evening, his throat was dry and scratchy. The next morning, he was sick enough for me to wonder whether to fly him to town and expose him to whatever else was out there in hopes the village clinic could help, or keep him home and take care of him myself.

Milt refused to go, so it was an easy decision.

I'd like to say I put him to bed and nursed him back to health with all the expertise I'd garnered through years of education and hospital nursing. But mostly he cured himself. He wouldn't hear of staying in bed after the first day. He just sucked on cinnamon fire sticks, gargled salt water, wrapped an extra scarf around his neck and went back to work.

For Better or for Worse

IN A LETTER to publisher Roy Reiman, Mariam Senger says, "When you write to Cora again, ask her to write another book...put in more everyday detail...such as where were they married—who performed the ceremony?"

HAPPILY EVER AFTER. Here we are, all together in December 1980, 16 months after the boys and I arrived at Chernofski, and a week after Milt and I were married.

HERE COMES THE BRIDE. We were married December 7, 1980 in Boise, Idaho at the St. Luke Medical Center because I admired the chaplain, Koji Hayant, pictured behind us (above). When I worked in Neonatal Intensive Care, he was helpful and caring with the suffering patients and nurses alike. I wanted our wedding to be warm and full of love, and in a small comfortable setting. Chaplain Hayant helped to make it all of those.

STRONG AS EVER. Although many things, both good and bad, have happened to us in the last 17 years, our marriage is as strong as it was the day we cut our wedding cake.

Creatures Great and Small

What kind of wildlife do you have on the island?
—*Warren Melcher, Murdo, South Dakota*

OUR LAND ANIMALS are limited to Aleutian red fox, the gray vole and an odd little hamster-like lemming, which we hardly ever see.

But our bay is full of marine life, and our skies teem with birds.

OUGHTA BE AN OTTER. Sea otters are more of a water creature than a land animal. But occasionally one will climb out onto the rocks to sleep in the sunshine.

PRETTY FOXY. The Aleutian red fox has little fear of strangers and allows us to come close, unless it is protecting a den of kits. This one (left) wasn't sure what to do, so it sat there while we took its photo.

MEOW? Sometimes our wildlife and our farm animals are hard to tell apart. Certainly "Harry", an orphan harbor seal, and the two cats in this photo don't seem to notice the difference. Harry is the one with the short hair, if anyone wonders.

KING OF THE COAST.
A bull sea lion guards his harem (above) near one of the rookeries that dot the coastlines of the Aleutian Islands. These are huge animals, and we leave them strictly alone. They have been known to jump onto boat decks and bite hands badly enough to require stitches. Sea lions are not part of our pet world.

STAY AWAY! A fur seal shared his rocks with wandering gulls but put on this menacing face (left) when surprised by intruders (us) who interrupted his nap in the sun.

ATTENTION! Murres, looking like little penguins, line the offshore rocks.

ROCKY FURBALL. This sea otter, more at home in the water, didn't seem to mind having its photo taken while sunning on the rocks.

DO IT TO SUET. Ruby-breasted finches and white Pribiloff buntings peck at the suet we put out in the winter.

A Place of Our Own

It all ended too soon! Page 274 brought the end to your interesting book. As the story of your life "after Boise" unfolded, we were intrigued by how you managed to become involved in the sheep ranch and the environment. Randall, Chuck and Milt blended so well, too, as you wrote, "Once a family, always a family".

What were your thoughts after making the decision to go so far from civilization? What was your reaction at arriving at the sheep ranch?   —Ray and Louise Bauer, Vienna, Virginia

AFTER I heard the words "The job is yours", I dropped the phone and grabbed Randall. We danced around the room chanting, "We're going to Alaska."

We were so excited that even when Chuck looked up the Aleutian Islands in the encyclopedia and found only one paragraph covering them, it didn't discourage us.

He read the Aleutians had been purchased from Russia along with Alaska, had been invaded by the Japanese during World War II, were sparsely populated by Aleuts and had an economy of subsistence fishing and isolated sheep ranches.

Russians! Indians! War territory! Fishing! A ranch with horses and boats and no school. What boy could resist such an adventure? They counted the days.

I longed for quiet…for beaches where I could walk forever…for a place where helpless babies didn't die at 3 a.m., where God was closer than the nearest church and where I could be a mom. I counted the days.

Like an omen, that October afternoon we landed in Chernofski Harbor was beautiful—a sunny windless day that left the bay a placid millpond.

The Grumman Goose touched down on the water and furrowed through it, sending up great plumes of spray that splashed the windows where our faces pressed. When the plane stopped and the water settled, I looked down. The water was so clear I could see the bottom, and it was covered with the most beautiful green stones. As I stared mesmerized at the shimmering pebbles, I suddenly had the strongest feeling that I had been here before.

When I climbed out of the plane and felt the damp sea breeze on my face and smelled the fresh salty air, I knew it was a homecoming. WOW!

CLEAR AND CALM. When I saw all this beauty the day I arrived, I knew right then I was home.

Earthquake!

I remember reading your description of an earthquake. Recently, our newspaper said the Aleutian Islands had an earthquake. I surely hope it didn't get close to you folks.

—Pauline Yost, Ten Sleep, Wyoming

IT SLAMMED into the house like a freight train, as I drifted in and out of sleep on a snowy January night in 1987. Milt had just come to bed after shutting down the light plant. Great, I thought. The wind is howling tonight.

Then noise exploded around us in a roaring rumble that rushed inside our bedroom. With it came the grinding of timbers and the screeching of wood. From a distance, with a dreamlike quality, I heard objects crashing into the walls and

RING OF FIRE. When Mount Tulik blew its top in 1945 (right), it showed why this area is part of the so-called "Ring of Fire".

114

rolling along the floor.

The bed lurched and bucked as I fought the covers in the dark. "Earthquake," I mumbled, reaching for Milt, still half asleep, and not yet comprehending that this might be the big one all of us on the Pacific "Ring of Fire" dread.

"Where is the danged flashlight?" Milt growled, hunting under his pillow as the bed tilted. His feet hit the floor and I heard him swear. I hadn't heard language like that since he came down the ladder from the attic and hit his tail bone on the door knob.

Recognizing the panic in his voice, I was jolted wide awake and realized we were having one terrible earthquake.

"I'm getting out of here!" I screamed, rolling off the sliding bed and falling on my knees behind it.

I heard a slight click and a tiny light beam lit the room. By its erratic glow, I saw the windows bulging in and out. The walls and ceiling buckled and rippled. Cabinet doors swung crazily open and banged back and forth, spewing their contents onto the floor where they rolled in all directions.

"Hey, you guys all right in there?" Chuck's high-pitched scream sounded from the next bedroom.

"Get in the doorway and stay there," Milt shouted. He flashed his feeble light over the clock—11:30 p.m. I crawled and staggered with him to the door and huddled there with my arms over my head, and biting back a hysterical desire to laugh as I pictured myself covered with hundreds of pounds of stored flour if the ceiling and attic gave way.

After the first jolt, the shudders came in waves, as if a giant dog had us gripped in his teeth and was flinging his head from side to side.

"This is serious, Milt," I gasped. "We better call someone and tell them what's happening while we still have a radio."

"Whoa," Chuck shouted. Instead of huddling in a doorway he was careening about the living room clad only in a shirt, which he had tied around his waist by the sleeves, and grabbing things as they toppled.

"Ah," he caught Milt's grandmother's fragile pottery elephant in mid-air then cannoned into the wall with it protected in his arms. "Yeah," he yelled. "The house is gonna fall down. Call the Coast Guard."

Milt's light wavered across the room throwing grotesque shadows on first one wall then another as the house lurched and heaved.

Static blared from the radio when Milt found the switch. "*Komstadt Kodiak*, this is WHV 727 Chernofski. We are having a severe earthquake."

More static issued from the speaker before a disembodied voice answered. "Coast Guard *Kodiak* back to the vessel calling. You are weak and barely readable. Please repeat."

I listened to Milt repeat his words while I fought panic by talking to myself. Do something, you idiot. Put on your arm. At least get dressed before you freeze to death.

Again static filled the room. "Sir, I repeat, you are weak and barely readable. Could you switch to 6238 for transmission and listen on 2670?"

My God, I thought, as I fumbled in the dark for my clothes, still not able to stand up. Right now I can't remember what comes after A. How can Milt even comprehend all those numbers.

As he searched the dials with his flashlight, another voice blared on the radio. "Hey, *Komstadt*, that was Milt out at Chernofski. He said they're having an earthquake."

Thank God. I started trembling. Somebody heard us.

Suddenly the radio came to life. "Milt, this is the *American Eagle*. Are you guys all right?"

"*Storm Petrel* calling Chernofski. I'm close if you need help. We didn't feel anything out here."

I swallowed a lump in my throat as others chimed in. Boats clamored for information from the Coast Guard. All had the same fear. Tsunami!

My head snapped to attention. Tidal wave! We were at sea level and less than 100 yards from the bay. What if it sloshed out like a spilled bowl of water. We'd be washed away. My fragile control shattered. From a distance, I heard myself start to whimper.

"Hey!" Chuck shouted, "it's letting up."

I staggered to my feet. The house still moaned and groaned all around us. But I could stand without falling. The roar didn't seem as loud.

"You're right," Milt said. "I think we can chance a lamp."

He steadied himself against the wall and struck a match. In the muted glow we saw everything from plants to books scattered around us.

The mess didn't even register as I listened to his voice, grateful that at least his calm had returned. "If we get a tidal wave it will be on the Pacific side and we'll only get the back wash through the pass. But we better be ready just in case. So get your coats on."

"How about Dutch Harbor, Milt?" I asked on a shaky breath. Randall had agreed to give high school in the village a try and was staying at the Jesse Lee home. It was right on the

CRATER CREEK. Okmok crater on Umnak Island (right) is 7-1/2 miles wide, big enough for this impressive river and waterfall.

beach road, even closer to the water than we were. "Will Randall be okay?"

"Don't worry," Milt said. "The minister is an old sailor. He'll know to get everyone out of there." He handed me a glove. "Now get wrapped up."

I tried to take his advice as we all dressed in freezer suits for the winter night. But worrying about Randall came natural to me and I wished he were back home.

The roar outside diminished to a faint rumble, and the giant dog's ferocious shake turned into a vigorous wag about every 3 minutes. We even attempted shaky smiles and I was about to suggest some hot cocoa when the radio screeched to life.

The Coast Guard was alerting all stations. Dutch Harbor was evacuating all boats and advising everyone to move back a mile from the beaches.

Citizens on the coast were advised to seek high ground in the event a

tsunami occurred. There followed a series of times when it would hit various places in the Aleutian coastal areas. We had 7 minutes.

In unspoken agreement we bolted for the door and rushed up the snow covered hillside behind the barn until we came to the upper warehouse.

For an hour we sat there while the wind wailed and blew the January chill through the thin walls. The aftershocks rattled through the structure with bone shaking strength as we sat there waiting for the one that didn't stop.

Chuck's voice sounded thin in a lull. "I wonder if this has any-

VOLCANIC SUNSETS. With Mount Tulik spewing steam and ash to the west, and Mount Macushin shooting off steam to the east, we here at Chernofski reap the benefits of gorgeous, colored clouds. This is a good part of having volcanoes as our neighbors here in the Ring of Fire. The earthquakes and threat of tsunamis, however, are not so romantic or gorgeous, even when they last only 17 seconds.

thing to do with Mt. Tulik and Mt. Macushin both steaming at the same time a couple weeks ago."

"Could be, I suppose," Milt answered and lapsed back into silence.

I jammed my hand, which was freezing despite a heavy glove, into the pocket of my freezer suit. "Well, whether it does or not," I declared, "we must be crazy to voluntarily live between two live volcanoes." My numb fingers encountered a forgotten candy bar.

"But think about the adventure," Chuck joked feebly.

"Hah," I exclaimed. "Don't tell me you weren't scared to death just like I was."

"Sure, I was scared," he admitted. "Still am, but not so scared I can't hear you unwrapping that candy bar in your pocket." He held out his hand.

I broke the slab of chocolate into three pieces and we shared it. When Milt finished he stood up and said. "Time to go."

We followed our footprints in the snow back to the barn, then stumbled through it and came out on the walk leading to the house. None of us mentioned the almost constant tremors.

As we neared the front gate, I wondered aloud, "Did that earthquake last 10 minutes?"

"Mom," Chuck exclaimed. "Don't be ridiculous."

"Well, how long then?" I asked him.

"No more than 5, tops," he assured me.

"More like 2," Milt added. "Time goes slower when you're terrified."

We got back in the house just in time for the all-clear announcement from the Coast Guard. Afterward, they read a news bulletin telling us the epicenter was 60 miles south of Unalaska Island in the North Pacific Ocean, and according to the National Weather Service Tsunami Warning Center in Palmer, Alaska, it measured 6.4 on the Richter Scale.

It lasted *17 seconds!*

A Picture Is Worth
A Thousand Words

SEVERAL READERS asked the same questions, so I've decided to answer these common queries with photographs. Here goes:

1. What is tundra?
FUNK AND WAGNALL'S dictionary defines tundra as a rolling, treeless, often marshy plain found in Siberia and Arctic North America. Chernofski Sheep Ranch is 13° of latitude south of the Arctic Circle so it doesn't fit all the criteria. But the countryside surrounding headquarters and the upper warehouse is rolling, treeless, and marshy.

2&3. *Do you get a lot of snow?*

OUR CLIMATE is maritime temperate, so we get more rain than snow, even in winter. But we average a couple good blizzards each year. The ranch buildings and yard show how less than a foot of snow gets blown into 6-foot drifts, slammed and frozen onto the walls, yet leaves the grass sticking through on the hillside.

Our weather follows a rough cycle and most snow is rained off within 10 days, making winter pasture available for stock.

4. *What are you doing for fun?*

CHUCK liked sliding down the hill in West Point pasture so much it was worth getting caught and scolded for wearing out his rain coat.

The Staff of Life

You mentioned that you order supplies every 2 years. What supply do you hate to run out of most?

I USED TO THINK the worst thing I could run out of was typing paper, but that was before I ran out of flour.

Most staples have a reasonable substitute. For example, macaroni works well in any pasta dish. Most dry beans are interchangeable. Rice makes a good carbohydrate whenever we run out of fresh potatoes. Brown sugar and honey replace granulated sugar. Baking powder and soda won't leaven as well as yeast, but it is possible to make bread with them.

I discovered, however, that nothing replaces plain old flour—especially not in sourdough pancakes, which is what Milt eats for breakfast every morning of his life.

Not rye, not cornmeal, not masa harina, not oatmeal, all of which I had. And definitely not 100 percent whole wheat pastry flour, which was what I had the most of.

In fact, that whole wheat pastry flour was the cause of my problem. In a 100-pound sack identical to my regular flour brand, except for the fine print, it masqueraded as my backup supply of unbleached white flour.

Secure in the knowledge I had enough to get me safely through till I ordered again, I made no effort to conserve. Down to the last 2 cups in my 25-pound canister, I sent Milt upstairs to replenish it. When he returned empty-handed and told me I didn't have any up there, I didn't believe him. "You can't miss it," I insisted.

"Go look," he invited.

With the evidence, or lack of, staring me in the face, I had to admit it. I had 2 cups of white flour and I hadn't made out my order yet. It would be months before I got more.

Okay, I thought, I'll improvise. How hard can it be to make 100 percent whole wheat bread? So I made a batch, and discovered it was a lot easier to make than it was to eat. It felt and looked like a brick. But I couldn't slice it without it crumbling into a hundred pieces.

Even worse than bread, whole wheat sourdough pancakes were not distinguishable from brake shoes.

I was astonished at the amount of flour almost every recipe took, from coating for meat, to thickening for gravies, to being the main ingredient in every dessert know to man.

If it had just been Milt here, it wouldn't have been so bad, but there was a fellow from Texas here breaking horses. Over the next few weeks, I came to dread anyone asking, "What's for supper?" or worse yet, "What's for breakfast?"

After the first few mornings, they stopped asking what it was, and I stopped asking how they liked it.

I was saved from actual mutiny, thanks to a host of *Country* readers who had shared some of their favorite local specialties with us by sending samples in the mail. We had one area in the attic full of these boxes, which I had been using sparingly to add variety to our meals. But if there was a time to be profligate, this was it.

So for one entire week, we breakfasted on Barbara Spitelera's Mardi Gras cake and beignets from New Orleans. What a treat! We developed quite a taste for those little square doughnuts with powdered sugar. Milt chose them every time over sourdough brake shoes.

For dinners, we feasted on Fair Isle scones from Washington State, sent by Doris Hannigen. Milton and our Texas cowboy, Sticker Wiggins, may have been a little prejudiced by their memory of my 100 percent cornmeal hockey pucks, because they declared those scones the best they'd ever tasted.

And I think I might just owe my life to James Warrick of Lancaster, Pennsylvania and Joyce Bemiller of Cape Coral, Florida. Their gifts of back-East delicacies contained big fat pretzels, crackers, cookies and various small mixes like gingerbread and date cake that saved my reputation as a cook for a whole month.

Every day I took time from searching through cookbooks for flourless recipes to get our supply order ready for the next plane, boat or pony-express rider who came past. And right at the top in great big letters, I wrote, "500 pounds of flour". I wasn't taking a chance on running out again.

We had a streak of luck when our first working vacationer of the year arrived by plane, and Randall's wife, Jennifer, sent out 50 pounds of flour from the village with her.

Just how lucky a break it was we didn't realize until a month later, when our supplies came in by boat and we discovered that our supplier had overlooked one zero on the manifest. Instead of 500 pounds of flour, he sent 50.

Still, I'm not too disappointed. Since sampling those mixes from all over the country, I decided to stock up on some. I may never start from scratch again. Or who knows, Milt may learn to like brake shoes and hockey pucks.

PUCK-MAKER. Thanks to "care packages" from readers, I didn't have to make any more hockey puck biscuits or brake shoe pancakes until my supply of flour arrived. But we developed a taste for those mixes.

Anything That Bites

You said your son was a fisherman. What kind of fish does he catch? —Dorothy Melcher, Murdo, South Dakota

CHUCK WAS 21 when he got his first job on a crab boat. He had no experience as a deckhand, so he hired on as cook for the *Spirit of The North*.

It was soon apparent that he had no experience cooking, either. But he was quick and agile and eager to learn crab fishing, so he was soon elevated to cook-deckhand.

That meant he worked pushing pots on deck until 20 minutes before mealtime, then he ran to the galley and threw something in the oven. From the way he tells it, his meals relied quite heavily on Stove Top Stuffing and instant rice.

At 21, Chuck was old to be getting into fishing. Most deckhands his age had been fishing since they were 16 or younger. He had a lot to learn, and the work was hard and dangerous. But he was used to that.

Crab pots were heavy and he knew they could fall on him if he didn't pay attention. But they didn't bite or kick when his back was turned.

After the first year of crab fishing in the Bering Sea, he saved enough to buy a small place in the village. During the following 2 years, he improved on it

ANGLING EARLY. Chuck's love affair with water and fishing began early. If there was water within walking distance, he would be there with his fishing pole.

between fishing trips, then sold it and bought a 32-foot boat.

For 3 years, he supported himself by fishing for halibut, cod and snow crab in and around Unalaska Bay. Money was never a priority for Chuck. He was his own boss, and he loved his life on the water. But changing regulations and shrinking fisheries closed many doors for small boat fishermen in Alaskan waters.

Instead of letting that defeat him, Chuck tied up his boat in April 1995 and again took a job as deckhand on a bigger boat, this time on a dragger out of Kodiak, fishing for pollack and gray cod.

LOOKS AREN'T EVERYTHING. No matter what it looks like, Chuck's boat is his castle. This weather-beaten little craft represents a way of life he loves.

LESSON LEARNED. Milt began teaching Chuck how to handle a small boat and read the water soon after we arrived at Chernofski. That knowledge was to prove invaluable when Chuck got older. When Chuck went out on his own, he was able to solve his transportation problems by using his 18-foot skiff (right) to get back and forth from the village, when the weather allowed it. On the island, everything is dependent upon the weather.

WHAT'S UP, DOCK? Tied to our dock (left), Chuck's boat looks too small and frail to do battle with the Bering Sea. But its sturdy wooden construction has kept it afloat since its christening in 1962, 3 years before Chuck was born! The two of them make a good pair, and Chuck would never give up the freedom the little boat provides.

WATER MOUNTAIN. Crab fishing in the Bering Sea means battling storms that create 50-foot waves like these (right) that tower over a boat, then break on top of it. This photo was taken from the wheelhouse of The Last Frontier.

HARD WATER. Big waves aren't the only thing Chuck has to face. In the winter, the water gets mighty hard to handle (below).

Dialing 911 at Chernofski

What do you do if you are sick or injured? —*Cheri Bennett*
Latrobe, Pennsylvania

WE DO the same thing everyone else does when they are sick or injured. We use the facilities available to us.

The closest hospital is 800 miles away in Anchorage, so that isn't an option. The clinic in Unalaska Village is 80 miles away, but in an emergency, it might as well be on another planet.

I'm a registered nurse, and I'm here, so our health and well-being mostly falls on my shoulders. I do what I can and leave the rest to God.

When we moved out here, we made the decision to take responsibility for our own lives. Since the boys were too young to really understand what that meant, I made the decision for them and thus felt doubly responsible for their safety.

But all the harping, hovering and hollering in the world can't prevent a boy and an accident from colliding, especially if that boy is Randall and the accident is explosive.

Because of the way we lived, very close together and dependent on each other, we tried to keep rules and regulations to a minimum. But the few we did have we expected everyone to obey.

By the time Chuck had gone adventuring in other parts of Alaska, Randall was 14 and so busy reloading cartridges, trapping fox and practicing with Milt's snowshoes that he hardly had time for classes, much less cleaning his room.

And that was one of the cardinal rules. When you couldn't shut your door because the mess in your bedroom was spilling out through the doorway, it was time to clean.

Between Christmas and February 1984, we were besieged with one blizzard after another and weather so cold Milt had a fire going in the radio room coal furnace day and night to keep us from freezing.

All three of us were fighting cabin fever. For several days, I had been nudging junk back through Randall's doorway and nagging him to get his room shoveled out.

He had been postponing the task with one excuse after another. But when Milt walked in to recheck a powder weight at Randall's request and stepped on a half-eaten sandwich, Randall decided to do some serious housekeeping.

We were in the third day of the blinding snowstorm that kept us all prisoners inside. So Randall worked away at his room all afternoon, then returned to it after supper.

"Looks like you're making real progress," I said, peeking in on my way to Chuck's old bedroom, which I had converted into a wool workroom because I could not stand to see his empty bed day after day.

"Yeah," Randall said enthusiastically. "All I have left is sweeping."

"Here's the broom." Milt dropped his magazine and brought the broom to Randall from the kitchen. "Couple hours with this and you'll be able to see the floor."

"Hah," Randall snorted. "Ten minutes. You watch me."
He wielded the broom furiously through the debris while Milt and I looked at each other and rolled our eyes.

I had just finished carding a batt of hand-spinning wool and was pulling it off the carder when I heard the heavy top lid of the radio room coal stove open. I added the batt to the others I had prepared and started back to the kitchen with them. I had just reached the door when...

KA BOOM!

Before I could react, I heard Milt's footsteps pounding on the floor. I dropped my wool and dashed around the corner of the living room just in time to see Randall land on the floor in front of our bedroom door, 8 feet from the black mushroom cloud billowing from the stove.

Milt bent over Randall, slapping and stomping. In a blur, I saw Randall lift his arms and cover his head. "What the...th..." I heard him stutter as he curled into a ball.

"You're on fire, son. Lie still." Milt brushed my hand away and continued to slap and stomp on the glowing coals that littered Randall's clothes and hair.

I dropped to my knees beside Randall's head and pinched out the smoldering spots in his shoulder-length hair. His eyes were open, two frightened circles in his soot-blackened face. His hair was singed close to his head. Both eyebrows were gone. He looked at me with the most bewildered expression.

"It's okay," I said. "We put all the fires out."

"What happened?" he croaked.

"You threw gunpowder in the stove and it exploded," Milt said in a matter-of-fact voice.

"Does it hurt?" I asked, peering closely at his skin. "Are you burned?"

"I...I...don't think so." Randall pushed against the floor with his hands and sat up, shaking his head dazedly. "It knocked me down." He touched his face. "I can't feel it."

"Thank God," I said. Reaction set in and my hands started to tremble. Then I got angry. "No more reloading," I snapped.

"You can thank your lucky stars you had on wool long johns," Milt growled as he helped Randall to his feet, brushing at scorched spots on the ancient underwear he had given Randall for his trap line trips. "They saved your bacon. Anything else would have burst into flame."

"Yeah," Randall looked down at the blackened material. "They're toasted," he joked feebly as he tried to undo them and the buttons popped off at his touch. "Ouch."

"What's wrong," I asked.

"Look," he said and held the stiffened material away from his chest. Six circular wounds marched down the midline of his torso.

I drew a shaky breath. The heat from the plastic buttons had burned holes in his flesh. "Those are third-degree," I said. "I want to look at your face; get in the bathtub and clean off the soot."

After he had gone, I looked at Milt. "What next?" I sighed. "Just when I think he has pulled every idiotic stunt under the sun, he comes up with something new."

"Now, Mom," Milt grinned. "What would we do for excitement if he wasn't here to liven things up?" He touched my cheek. "But I'll admit that was enough for one night. I'll lay the kitchen fire and stir up the sourdough while you fix his burns, then I'll get the lights turned off...if I can get the door open." He returned to the kitchen.

In the upheaval, I had forgotten the blizzard. Glancing out a bedroom window I passed on my way to the cubbyhole for first aid supplies, I saw it was covered by snow.

I was rummaging in the usual clutter for Furacin ointment when I heard sobs coming through the connecting wall.

I bolted for the bathroom and wrenched at the locked door. "Let me in," I shouted.

"It hurts!" he shrieked. "It hurts!"

"Open up the door." I rattled the knob. "Come on."

"I'm naked," he whimpered. "I can't."

"I promise I won't look," I coaxed. "Just let me in."

The lock clicked and I knocked the door out of my way as Randall dove back into the tub. "What hurts?" I demanded, leaning over his huddled form.

"My face and neck," he cried. "The warm water hurts."

He jerked away from my hand and emitted a high keening wail as I touched his cheek. I stuck my face close to his and saw where tears had put streaks in the soot, leaving a trail of red blistered skin.

As the steam from his bathwater loosened the soot, I could see the blisters emerging on his cheeks and the soft skin under his chin. Realizing these burns called for more than Furacin, I dashed into the cubbyhole and grabbed a precious jar of Silvadene from our marine medical chest.

Without a thought to its cost, I smeared the soothing white cream liberally over Randall's face and neck right over the soot.

"Close your eyes," I commanded. As I worked, I saw small tremors course across his shoulders. The tissue of his throat swelled under my hands. "Get out of the water," I told him.

I handed him a towel. "I'll be right back."

"Hurry," he whispered hoarsely. "I'm scared."

In the kitchen, I interrupted Milt's fire building. "He has burns on his face and neck, too," I blurted.

"How bad?"

"I'm afraid his throat will swell shut."

Milt looked up, astonished. "Oh, surely not."

"I know it seems impossible," I quavered. " But I can see it puffing up and he is so scared. I got out an airway and a flash-light, but I don't have a laryngoscope."

My own throat closed. "And I don't know if I could do a tra-cheotomy on my own son. I guess if he was turning blue..." My voice trailed off.

Milt just stared at me. "I need something to keep the edema down and take away the pain," I whispered. "I wish I had some ice."

Milt dropped the kindling he was arranging in the firebox. "Go back to Randall," he said.

I don't know how he did it, because later it took us both to open the door when we finally felt the danger was past enough to turn out the lights. But I hadn't been back with Randall more than 5 minutes when Milt brought us a dishpan full of snow.

Together, Milt and I took care of Randall. We talked constantly while we changed the packs, reassured him for hours that every-thing was fine, kept him warm with blankets and later put him to bed with two codeine tablets. But it was the snow packed in damp towels around his neck that kept him from choking.

After he was asleep and we had gotten the lights turned off, I dozed beside his bed with a fresh pan of snow. When he fell asleep around 3 a.m., I crawled into bed beside Milt. "He's go-ing to be all right," I mumbled.

By morning, he was much improved. The swelling had sub-sided and the cold had taken the painful fire out of the burns. When I unwrapped the gauze from his face, it peeled away the Silvadene and soot. Randall's cheeks and neck were a mass of blisters and raw flesh.

"You're going to live," I said, my severe tone masking utter relief. "But I think you can forget about growing a beard."

CLEAN-SHAVEN SHAVER. My prediction about Randall not being able to grow a beard proved to be true. By 19, he still had managed only a mustache, as his upper lip had somehow escaped the blast from the gun-powder. Except for that, the only other reminder of that frightening day is a very red face whenever it gets cold.

The Second Most Asked Question

Do you ever leave the island, go visit family, take a vacation?

LIKE MOST RANCHERS, we keep close to home because of our livestock responsibilities. We never leave unless we have a pressing need, and that's nearly always medical.

TOGETHER AGAIN. Recovering from his first total hip-replacement surgery in 1977, Milt attended a family reunion with his brother, Tom, and sisters, Leanor, Peggy and Mildred. He hadn't seen any of them since 1959, when he came back for his father's funeral. With his beard, long hair and hat, Milt seemed a bit out of place with his more cosmopolitan family. But they still remain close and keep in regular contract with yearly letters. We're a long way from our families, we know, but when we see them again, it's a true reunion and a time for real celebration.

ANOTHER HIP REUNION. In 1983, when Milt had his second hip replacement, we took the opportunity to attend my Gorley family reunion in Boise, Idaho. Milt is easily identified, again, by his crutches and trademark hat. This time, he was as clean-shaven as when I met him. But I liked the beard, so he let it grow back again.

CENTENNIAL CELEBRANTS.
When the end of Milt's mandatory convalescence coincided with Idaho's centennial ball, we couldn't miss the chance to dress up and attend (left). Only those who know Milt realized that I was the only one wearing a costume! At least this time, Milt was without his crutches.

MILT'S TWIN SISTER gave him a big hug at their 1990 reunion (right). We were back for Milt's fourth hip surgery, so Mildred had to work around the crutch.

CRUTCHLESS VACATION. We really enjoyed ourselves the one time Milt and I took a vacation. It was to attend Randall and Jennifer's wedding in Eureka, California. I felt so strange being outside Alaska with my husband on two feet that I was constantly looking around for his crutches.

Family Ties

Do any of your family visit?

LET'S DO LUNCH. If my sister Alice Triplett (left) loves anything better than catching fish, it's eating them. She'd never fished anything but streams before, so our bay was a constant source of delight, with its huge and wondrous species. How much does she like fish? During her 3-week stay, Alice ate this entire halibut!

RIGHT ON SCHEDULE. When Milt and his twin sister, Mildred, turned 70, Mildred's husband, Tony Howard, decided to surprise her with a trip to Chernofski. Tony knew how difficult travel was to this area, so he began planning for the August trip in April. That was a good thing, because when Val helped Mildred off the plane and into Milt's arms (below), they were only 23 days late!

BEAUTIFUL BOULDERS. When my sister Doris and her husband, Jose Tellcria, visited in 1988, they, too, fell in love with the island. Despite almost constant rain for their entire stay, they explored every beach within walking distance and were drawn to this stretch of boulder-strewn beauty, with its "glory hole" above it. From above, these openings in the rock are sometimes camouflaged with grass and easy to stumble into.

PEBBLE PICNIC. Although crippled by polio when she was a young woman, Milt's mother, Ruth, was able to spend the summer of 1965 at Chernofski. Here she shares a picnic with Val and Mary. Val, decked out for the occasion in his raccoonskin cap, has the marshmallows handy, should the fire ever get started. Meantime, Grandma is waiting.

"I CAN DO IT." It looks like Chuck should be giving his 79-year-old grandmother a hand getting aboard his boat. But he knows better. This was Grandma Gorley's second trip to the ranch, and she was an old hand at boat boarding.

GRANDMA AND THE GOOSE. By the time Grandma Gorley had been to the ranch four times, she had even taken flying in the Grumman Goose in stride. There was still that dinky ladder to climb down, and that was a little tricky. But Grandma has been through a lot, including being locked in our greenhouse.

Accent on Alaska

Do you speak with an accent? —*Cheri Bennett*
Latrobe, Pennsylvania

IF ANYONE had asked us that a few years ago, I would have said "No, we just talk regular American." But we've had some guests who sure talk funny.

Like the fellow from Texas, Sticker Wiggins, who was breaking horses. We could hardly understand a word he said.

Julie Habel, the *Country* photographer from Iowa, talked much differently than we do. And we had a working vacationer from New Jersey, Josephine Holmes; although I understood her well enough, her speech had a decided Eastern accent.

Did I sound as strange to them as they did to me? I don't know. But I've never had anyone say, "Oh, my. You must be from Alaska. I can tell by your accent."

Watching the Clock

How do you keep track of time? Or does time of day mean much?
—*Esther Simco, Newark, Ohio*

WE OWN A CLOCK, and it helps us remember what day it is, because on Sunday, we have to wind it.

Sometimes we have a calendar, sometimes not, especially for the first few months of the New Year.

The way we keep accurate track of time is by keeping a daily diary. Milt is steadfast in jotting down the temperature and wind direction along with a short account of his activities.

There is never enough time. We mourn its passing the same way you do. It slips through our fingers just as fast as if we were watching a clock.

After all these years, our routine is simple. We sleep when it's dark and we work while it's light. Sometimes, if there isn't enough light, we work in the dark, but we rarely sleep in the light.

We eat breakfast when we get up and we eat dinner whenever we get hungry, or whenever we get back to the house from whatever we are doing.

Besides daylight and dark, high and low tides are important to us. We follow their rough 6-hour schedule, because it behooves anyone who lives around the water to pay attention to tides. When we were riding constantly during the summer rounding up livestock, we lived by daylight, darkness and the tides.

While I rode, a prayer ran though my mind like a constant litany. "Dear God, help us get these cattle back across the flats before the tide comes in, and then help us get them behind the Cutter Point fence before dark." Sometimes He did.

Utopia? Not by a Long Shot!

The sibling rivalry between your boys must have been trying, not to mention the mischief. I have two boys in their early 50's, and they still tell me things they did as youngsters that my husband and I sure wouldn't have approved of. I guess boys will be boys.   —*Esther Simco, Newark, Ohio*

WHEN I STARTED writing *Good-Bye, Boise...Hello, Alaska*, I debated how much to downplay the friction between Chuck and Randall.

I wanted my book to be as authentic as possible and an accurate portrayal of our life here on the ranch. Since the bickering and fighting between Chuck and Randall was a big part of our early years, I knew I needed to include it.

From the response we've received from hundreds of parents who struggled through the same crisis years as we did, I know I made the right choice. A true story demanded reality, and the book would have lacked credibility without it.

The anger the boys expressed made my heart sad. In fact, I despaired many times that my sons would always be enemies.

Nothing caused me more heartbreak than admitting to myself that two of the people I loved best in world hated each other—at the tops of their voices most of the time.

I felt helpless and inadequate and stupid and angry. Yet, even at my most defeated, when I wanted nothing more than to wring both their necks, Milt was always there to keep us on an even keel. "We have lots of time," he'd say.

So, one day after another, the four of us made it through some very tough times. And every one of them was worth it in the lesson it taught, even though the reason wasn't always apparent until much later.

Several years ago, Chuck visited us and suddenly asked Milt, "How did you stand us?"

"I knew it wasn't going to last," he told him.

And it didn't. The boys have grown up enough to accept their differences and appreciate them. Randall is still a determined workaholic and Chuck a sensitive dreamer. Nothing will change that.

But the last time I saw Randall, when he skiffed to the ranch for his 26th birthday in May, he brought a video of himself baking a cake for Chuck's 30th birthday, which they celebrated together.

Six weeks later, Chuck came down in his fishing boat, and while we were visiting, he said the words I'd been waiting half a lifetime to hear. "That Randall, I'm proud he's my brother."

And, yes, sometimes they still hate each other at the tops of their voices.

BROTHERLY LOVE. *Chuck and Randall had their differences when they were young. They still do, but they now accept those differences and appreciate them.*

Students Have Questions

I send you warm greetings from the Czech Republic. I suppose you don't know anything about this small country in middle Europe, but I know something about you from Country magazine. I'm a teacher of English at a grammar school. My students don't have much possibility to write in English abroad and they have been amazed to write you some words. They are 15 years old. —Renaia Ulman, Krnov, the Czech Republic

May 26, 1994 from Gymnazium 1.A:

"We are writing this letter at 9 o'clock. We have got English language."

"We are from the Czech Republic. It is a small country in the heart of Europe. Its capital city is Prague. We adjoin Poland, Germany, Austria and Slovakia. The Czech Republic has about 10 million people."

"There are many castles where some rulers ruled. These castles stand up for miles, but they are only for tourists. Many strangers admire these castles."

"Today is in our country democratic government with president."

"Our republic national food is dumpling, cabbage and pork."

"We attend grammar school like American high school, 4 years."

"In summer we play hockey and in autumn we play football. There are nice athletic stadiums. We play football very much, namely boys and girls."

"We live in the small town of Krnov. It is in the north of our country. The population is 27,000. Krnov is an old town. Town hall was founded in the 12th century."

Renaia's Students from the Czech Republic are curious about Chernofski Sheep Ranch and have plenty of questions. They want to know:

How often is there snow? Off and on from October to June.

Do you believe in God? Yes.

Are there forests on the island? No.

Have you ever been in Europe? No.

How large is your herd of cattle? 1,400 head.

WORLD OF QUESTIONS. Even from halfway around the world, people have heard of Chernofski, are fascinated by it and want to know more about it.

How many helpers do you have? None, except volunteers in the summer.

Are you interested in politics? Not really.

How often is there sun? An average of 8 days a year.

How often do you go to the shops? We shop by catalog.

Where do your sons go to school? They took correspondence courses. Randall went to Sitka, Alaska for one year of high school and to Dutch Harbor, Alaska for another.

What is your weather like? Our maritime temperate climate means we have cool damp weather with an average of 40° year-round.

What food do you like best? Lamb.

Did your ancestors live on Unalaska? No.

Does any of your family live on the island and visit you? Randall, Chuck and Milt's youngest son, Val.

Do you read any newspapers? Not often. We keep up on world news by listening to Voice of America on the shortwave radio every day at 1 a.m.

Are you missing society of other people? Not really. We miss our children when they aren't here.

What animals live there? Aleutian red fox, gray vole and gold-colored lemming.

Have you ever been to Africa? No.

What are the names of your dogs? "Hank", "Dusty", "Puck" and "Lilli Belle".

Porridge and Potatoes

Do you and your family celebrate the holidays? If you cook favorite recipes, list a few.   —Lois Brotherton, Alma, Arkansas

TWO SPECIALTIES at Chernofski Sheep Ranch make cooking easy. These dishes make an appearance every day rather than just on holidays, which we celebrate by taking the day off.

Milt's Porridge (No breakfast would be complete without it)
Ingredients:
    2 cups water in a shallow pan (water no more than 1 inch deep)
    Pinch of salt
    Handful of raisins
    Handful of coarsely chopped nuts.
    2 handfuls of old-fashioned oatmeal (thick-cut if possible)
Bring water, salt, raisins and nuts to a boil. Sprinkle oatmeal evenly over the water; shake pan gently to distribute. Simmer on back of stove for 10 minutes or until water is absorbed. Serve hot with cream and brown sugar. Serves 2.

Crispy Fried Potatoes
Ingredients:
    2 medium potatoes, grated, rinsed in cold water and drained
    Salt and pepper to taste
    Bacon fat or cooking oil
Choose a big enough cast-iron skillet so layer of potatoes is 1/4 inch thick in bottom of pan. Heat generous coating of fat on hot stove until it starts to smoke. Slide potatoes into pan and pat into an even layer with spatula. Sprinkle with salt and pepper. Cook undisturbed on medium hot stove 7 minutes or until the bottom is golden brown. Loosen by shaking skillet back and forth. If potatoes stick, slide spatula gently under them until they move freely in a single mass. Grasp skillet handle in both hands and flip potatoes with a quick jerk of your wrists. Catch potatoes in hot skillet and cook another 5 minutes or until underside is golden brown. Serve with catsup. Serves 2.

Mail Call

It sounds cool in Alaska. I'm home-schooled and in seventh grade. Is it true you only get mail a couple times a year?
—Bob Lou Arnaud, Shelby, Montana

SOMETIMES it seems like it, Bob Lou. For people used to getting daily mail, our erratic and frequently nonexistent service would be frustrating.

Milt recalls that it was hard getting used to no mail service, after having monthly deliveries from 1948 until the mid-1970s. Chernofski was dropped from the scheduled mail route then. Today, passing plane pilots and boat captains deliver mail out of the goodness of their hearts.

When crab fishing was good around Unalaska Island, our mail service was almost regular, every 8 to 10 weeks.

From 1982, when crab seasons closed, to 1992, when we began offering working vacations, we averaged between four and six mail deliveries a year. That means we often went as long as 4 months without seeing another human being, much less one with a mailbag over his shoulder.

Now, working guests, whose first task is collecting our mail on their way through the village, arrive once a month during the summer.

Winter mail deliveries are far between. But either Chuck or Randall tries to be home for Christmas, and they always bring the mail. They know their Christmas presents will be in it!

SPECIAL DELIVERY. Any time mail comes, it's special. Even the pet lamb helps unload.

'DEAR CORA...'

In letters and personal photos, American veterans of World War II's Aleutian campaign remember Chernofski.

Editor's Note: Cora Holmes dedicated her first book, *Good-Bye, Boise...Hello, Alaska*, to all the young men who served in the Aleutian Islands during World War II.

"Your legacy of freedom will always be part of Chernofski," she wrote. "Wherever you are now, I hope you enjoy reading about, and perhaps recognizing, locations that haven't changed in the last half century."

The military left Chernofski Harbor in the late 1940s, and indeed, little has changed since then. From the coal that warms Milt and Cora's home, to the roads they use, to the relics of docks, Quonset huts and cold storage buildings around their ranch, the Holmeses are reminded daily of their island's military past.

Cora's writing is often filled with genuine empathy for the lonely boys who once huddled against the cruel winds in their flimsy tents, deeply scared and longing for home.

The letters that follow were sent to Cora by many of those boys, now American veterans who recall the Aleutians of 60 years ago. Their photographs and memories are included here as a tribute to their courage.

WARM AGAIN. When this photo was taken in 1944, Harrel Chancellor was back home on the Arkansas farm where he lives today.

I AM one of the GIs who left you the coal.

I was a 21-year-old platoon sergeant in the 37th Infantry when we landed at Dutch Harbor, just 6 hours before the Japanese attacked us twice in 2 days.

I heard a story about a pilot of a PBY, who was flying back from a bombing run on Kiska when a pelican landed on his wing. He said, "I just set the plane down on the water. I knew if it was too rough for a pelican to fly, it was for me, too!"

—*Harrel Chancellor*
Huntsville, Arkansas

I WAS drafted into the Army in May 1942. On October 12, we sailed for Alaska, one place I'd always wanted to go.

We stopped first in Dutch Harbor, then Chernofski Bay. On Thanksgiving there, the wind blew so hard that I had to hold my pancakes down with my mess gear spoon to keep them from blowing away.

—*Charles Bockstruck*
Hillsboro, Illinois

HUT HOME. Charles Bockstruck lived in this Quonset at Amchitka.

154

WHILE STATIONED at Chernofski Bay in 1943 and '44, I helped build the dock and cold storage plant there. I was with B Company of the 802nd Aviation Engineers.

I went fishing in a creek for steelhead trout. There is a copper vein on the left side as you go upstream. I also remember a 12-foot-high falls not far from the bay.　　—*Thomas Langan*
Nucla, Colorado

WE LANDED in Chernofski Bay in late January 1942. I remember the sheep ranch house and barns across the bay from where we landed.

I was a sergeant in the engineers, and we built a small dock and a road around the bay. Later on, we built a bigger dock and some storage warehouses.　　—*Bill Mattas*
Carson City, Nevada

I SPENT 28 months on Unalaska and Umnak Islands during World War II.

We landed at Chernofski Bay in the latter part of January 1942. There were about 4,000 of us.

We pitched our eight-man tents about 30 feet from the ocean. Even though the tents were pinned down with 4-foot stakes, the stiff winds kept blowing them over.

In the center of each tent was a little Sibley stove, which was almost worthless. Besides the Japanese, the weather was our worst problem.

It was my responsibility to order C rations for all the troops. The Army decided to bury a lot of C rations in case the enemy came. They're still buried there near the bay, I'm sure.

After 4 months at Chernofski, I transferred to Umnak. There were no docking facilities there, so they barged supplies across the 13 sea miles from Chernofski with a powerful tug.

One time, I saw a large barge loaded with Army trucks being towed across. The seas were terribly rough, and the tug was having trouble making headway. Finally, the tug cut the cable and abandoned the barge. It drifted over and broke up on Ship's Rock, near Umnak.

Later, I went back to Chernofski Bay. By then, a number of Quonset huts and wooden buildings had been erected.

—Elden Bass, Loup City, Nebraska

I'M WRITING this letter with lots of sadness for not being able to return to Chernofski Bay. I spent 2 years there.

I landed at Chernofski in June 1942. Though there were no trees, everything was green and the valleys were filled with flowers.

Tears flowed when I read your stories about this wonderful place. *—George Gatcomb, Bradford, Maine*

I WAS a brief visitor to Chernofski during World War II.

In early fall of 1944, I was in charge of the Navy's weather station and forecast center at Dutch Harbor. While visiting the weather station on Umnak Island, I was delayed by heavy fog and stormy weather. I finally took passage on a small supply vessel.

We arrived at Chernofski Harbor near dark, in heavy rain. I found a bunk that night at one of the ranch buildings. As I recall, a number of civilian employees were there in addition to the couple in charge.

I'll never forget the beautiful wildflowers of late spring

WEATHER'S FINE. Lieutenant (junior grade) Thurlow Pitts forecast the weather. He posed at Amchitka Island Weather Center in January 1944.

and summer! We envied one of the intelligence officers who took pictures with color film.

Earlier, awaiting transportation from Seattle, I was told I'd like the Aleutians very much—a woman behind every tree! You know what I found.   —*Thurlow Pitts, Stonington, Maine*

I WAS STATIONED at Chernofski and Umnak Island from May 1942 through May 1944. During this time, Dutch Harbor was bombed and I witnessed an aerial dogfight between Japanese planes and ours.

For about 4 months in spring of 1944, I was stationed at the entrance to Chernofski Bay, operating one of the searchlights.

We were dug in on the high point, facing the Pass and the Bering Sea. The light itself was stored in the side of a knoll so it could be rolled out when in use. The motor to furnish the power was dug in a short distance away.

We used the light to search for enemy subs, but more often, it was used to guide ships coming into the harbor. We kept it on for

IOWA CONTINGENT. Harold Barlow (left above) and his buddies, Charles Milg, Burdette Voss and Oscar Moen, all Iowa boys, spent 1942 and 1943 on Umnak Island.

only 10 or 15 minutes at a time, as it had to cool down. It was out for most of the night.

I'll never forget our "bathroom facilities". They were simply two boards nailed together facing the bay. There was no cover. All the ships coming into the bay were in plain sight, and I'm sure we looked pretty funny sitting out there in the open.

          —*Harold Barlow, Nashua, Iowa*

I REMEMBER the williwaws that blew through the Aleutians and how the snow would be driven through every crack. It would completely fill the engine compartments of any vehicle left outdoors.

I remember how the wind would blow the snow horizontally across the ground and make the visibility zero. We had ropes strung between our Quonset huts and the latrine so we wouldn't get lost in the blinding snow.

—William Johnson
Summerville,
Pennsylvania

SNOWY MEMORIES. William Johnson recalls this heavy snowfall on Umnak Island.

IT'S GREAT to hear from somebody who lives on the island I was on during World War II.

We were in the coast artillery, and I was a .50-caliber machine gunner. There were 2 or 3 dozen Aleut Indians who were temporarily sent to the mainland for safety.

AT THE READY. Forrest Grimes (above on .50-caliber machine gun) luckily didn't see any air raids at Chernofski...but the other side of the island did!

I still have several native spearheads and fish hooks. Whenever the tide receded, it would uncover them.

We were up there 2 years and 2 months, but it seemed like an eternity. There wasn't much to do except stand guard and play cards.

—Forrest Grimes
Greensburg, Indiana

CHERNOFSKI AT WAR. Chernofski Harbor was a busy place in 1942 when Forrest Grimes took this photo. There was always the threat of a Japanese attack.

DURING World War II, I was stationed on Umnak as an assistant program director for the American Red Cross Service Club.

In August 1944, I visited the people at Chernofski Sheep Ranch. Their home was very modest and small.

I remember the winds, which we called "williwaws". We played a game of leaning into them and seeing how long they'd hold us up.

I also remember fog that swirled around you so thick, you couldn't see your feet when you looked down.

One other memory—I made a specific point of wading in the Bering Sea, just to say I'd done it.   *—Maryl Livingston*
Mt. Vernon, Washington

IN 1942, I was with the Army, and our campsite was on a small peninsula in Chernofski Harbor. It was called Otter's Point. We lived in tents and used a wooden panel mess hall.

We found small relics like carved figurines, which made us

think a native village had been there some years before.

Across the bay from our campsite, we could see an old shed or barn, and some type of living quarters. We were told a sheep rancher lived there, but were never allowed to go over there. —*Hugh Godwin, Clarkston, Georgia*

THE YEAR of 1942, we debarked at Chernofski, arriving from Seattle. We were taken to Umnak on cattle scows. It was a harrowing ride in rough waters; we were seasick, cold and soaking wet.

We spent 18 months up there, and I recall we adopted a lot of cute blue fox puppies. They'd eat Army C rations right out of our hands.

Please send me a few blades of grass from the tundra. I'll cherish them for the memories. —*Frank Szafranski*
Dolton, Illinois

I RECALL one or more large metal Quonset huts that sat on the narrow strip of low land between Chernofski Bay and the Bering Sea. The motor pool was there and probably a warehouse.

On clear days, looking across Unalaska toward Dutch Harbor, you could always see a wisp of steam rising from one of the mountain peaks.

In June of 1942, I was a 22-year-old boarding a troop ship in Seattle. We weren't told where we were going, and several days later, our ship pulled into the bay at Chernofski. Over the next 27 months, I'd learn much about the Aleutian Islands —Unalaska, Umnak, Adak, Kisaka, Attu...

I SHALL RETURN? Lester Myers posed at Chernofski in 1943. He visited the Holmeses' ranch in 1995.

I was a radar operator in the 503rd Coast Artillery. Our radar at Chernofski Bay was on the high bluff overlooking the Bering Sea to the north. We remained until 1943, when we moved to Attu.

My best memories of my Aleutian tour are of the Chernofski Bay radar site. I'll never forget the foxes and caribou on the islands. — *Lester Myers, Marquard, Missouri*

OUR field artillery unit was headed for Guadalcanal when central intelligence decoded a Japanese message. They were on a two-pronged attack—one toward Midway, the other toward Dutch Harbor. We re-routed to the North Pacific.

We were supposed to land at an island further west, but during a storm, one of my buddies fell off a top bunk and broke his arm.

The only hospital in the Aleutians was at Dutch Harbor, and we were trying to put him ashore there when "friendly" planes approached. Suddenly, bombs began falling all around us!

A destroyer escorted us out of the harbor—and right between two Japanese aircraft carriers! I think the Good Lord was taking care of us that day, because a thick fog helped us tremendously. The destroyer escorted us to Chernofski Bay and safety. — *Bert Triemstra Kalamazoo, Michigan*

LIFESAVER. Bert Triemstra and his pals rescued this caribou just as the waves were about to pull it out to sea.

I SPENT most of 1953 working for the Navy as a civilian seaman operating tugs and FS boats out of Kodiak.

I've probably visited every port in the Aleutians, including your elongated bay at Chernofski. I've ducked in there many times to escape the fierce winds blowing down from the North Pole across the Bering Sea.

The last time I was in that harbor, there was a lengthy dock, at least a half mile long. There were many cold storage warehouses and barracks.

One time, we ducked into Akutan Harbor when the seas were too rough. No sooner had we tied up when a whale boat full of Aleuts came to pay us a visit.

They seldom saw outsiders and invited us to a dance at the school that evening. Everyone in the village turned out, and a delightful time was had by both the native Aleuts and the ship's crew. —*Richard Hansen, North Bend, Oregon*

I WAS one of the first Navy nurses assigned to the dispensary at Dutch Harbor in 1943.

We were very busy in the dispensary, but we had time for other activities.

We visited Unalaska Village sometimes. I recall a small store where we made some purchases at a premium. We enjoyed a picnic in the Mukushin Valley on a misty day, and

NAVY NURSES Bernice Gorski (seated) and Mary Ellen MacIntosh paused while hiking on Unalaska in 1943.

it was fun to watch the trout in the streams.

One of the most beautiful sights I recall was when some pilots took me for a plane ride. We circled the active volcano, and the sight of the sun going down in pink cloud formations is something I will never forget. —*Bernice Gorski*
Doylestown, Pennsylvania

MY VISIT to Chernofski on March 2, 1945 started with a horrendous boat ride from Umnak Island on a BSP (barge self-propelled) boat.

The trip lasted perhaps an hour in rough seas, and I ended up in someone's bed. I recall dishes tumbling out of their holders and crashing to the floor. I don't remember how long we were on Chernofski or how rough the trip back to Umnak was. I probably blacked out! —*Frank Carnes*
Ormond Beach, Florida

WELL-TRAVELED SERGEANT Frank Carnes served in Alaska's interior as well as the Aleutians. He photographed the Russian church in Dutch Harbor in 1945.

I WAS at Chernofski Bay as a member of an Army Port Corps during the winter of 1944. On Christmas Day, it was unusually warm. There was no snow and you didn't need a jacket.

—*Reginald Strout, Brewer, Maine*

WARM CHRIST-MAS. There was no white Christmas for Reginald Strout at Chernofski in 1944...and a mighty short tree!

I REMEMBER the williwaws, the fog and the storms of the Aleutian Chain, where I was stationed from 1942 to 1944. I was assigned to a radar/loran radio weather station.

On Umnak, we recorded a gale of 150 mph before the anemometer blew away. A partially completed Quonset hut and a bunch of empty oil barrels blew clear across the island, into the Pacific, 5 miles away.

—*Archer Merrick Norton, Ohio*

HOW WINDY WAS IT? Too windy for Archer Merrick one day on Umnak Island.

IN 1942, I was a 22-year-old in the U.S. Army. I belonged to the 807th Aviation Engineer Company, and we set up camp in Chernofski Harbor as an advance unit to build an airfield on Umnak Island.

We camped near a small sand beach, where we dug many ivory artifacts out of the sand. This led me to believe Chernofski was a favored gathering place for the natives years ago.

I worked on a 75-foot towboat ferrying supplies between Unalaska and Umnak. Once we went over to pick up an empty barge, and I didn't think we'd make it back.

We couldn't find the entrance to the harbor in the blizzard and broke radio silence for help.

BROTHERS IN BUCKSPORT. Ben Craig (right) was back home in Maine with his brother Edward, a Marine. They hadn't seen each other in 6 years.

The wind was blowing directly out of the harbor and we were climbing unbelievable waves the size of mountains.

The gunboat *USS Charleston* always lay at anchor in the narrow harbor entrance checking all incoming and outgoing traffic. We passed within feet of that ship, and we never saw them, nor they us. —*Ben Craig, Bucksport, Maine*

MY HUSBAND, Sergeant Reig Green, lived on Unalaska for 27 months in the early 1940s.

A large flock of sheep was being tended there. I don't know

if the Army paid for them or simply conscripted them, but Reig said they ate lots and lots of mutton. In fact, he told me never to serve him lamb or mutton again. He'd his fill on Unalaska.

—*Ruth Green, Olsburg, Kansas*

I WAS a nurse stationed on Umnak during World War II. Four of us hitched a ride over to the ranch on a beautiful summer Sunday in 1945.

HORSELESS MOWER. Charlotte Doornbos enjoyed her visit to the Chernofski ranch in 1945. Not only was it a rare sunny day, she got all the fresh milk she could drink.

Mrs. Catron had saved all the extra cow's milk, so we drank fresh milk all day, then took 10 gallons back to our kitchen.

They had horses saddled for us and ready to ride. I remember a small stream that was so full of salmon they covered the bed completely.

—*Charlotte Doornbos, Belgrade, Montana*

YOUR STORY takes me back to 1943, when we put ashore at Chernofski.

While we awaited another troop ship, a sheep rancher from across the bay asked the military command for some GI volunteers with ranching experience.

I was among four who volunteered, though the closest thing to ranching I'd ever done was picking peas and beans in western New York.

Only one of us knew which end of the horse the bridle belonged on. It must have been pretty obvious to the rancher that we were one sad-sack bunch of cowboys, as he watched us try to get a team harnessed and saddle some tundra broncs.

Luckily, the project wasn't all cowboying. We separated the rams from the ewes and helped string fence.

I especially remember the beauty and tranquillity of the 6-8 mile ride to the jobsite. The trail traversed a stream alive with salmon. There were eagles galore and

BEFORE MILT, Mr. and Mrs. Catron ran the ranch. They are recalled by many World War II vets, including Reginald Strout, who took this photo in '44.

beside the stream were fish drying racks, presumably left by the Aleuts who were evacuated when hostilities began.

—*George Romance, Show Low, Arizona*

DURING my military service, I was stationed on Umnak Island, just across from Chernofski Bay. I also served as a clerk at port headquarters at Chernofski. We handled all the freight routed to Umnak.

I experienced several williwaws of 175 miles per hour. At one time, I had a photo of me feeding a red fox from my hand and holding a young eagle on my gloved hand. We enjoyed what we called "wild strawberries", which we found on the tundra during summer. My buddies and I went fishing and caught a halibut. I haven't tasted halibut that good since.

—George Venable, Albany, Oregon

ONE OF MY BUDDIES found a kayak in Nikolski. He did okay paddling it, but when I tried, it was a disaster.

I got in and he pushed me off. Suddenly, I found myself looking up at the sea urchins. That water is *cold.*

—Archer Merrick, Norton, Ohio

I WAS already in the Army when America entered the war. In December 1941, we were ordered to Alaska.

During the time I was at Chernofski, the sheep ranch operators would occasionally visit us. After the Japanese bombed Dutch Harbor, the Army evacuated the sheep ranchers. They returned before we left for reassignment in 1944.

—Donald Weisert, Jesup, Iowa

BOOTS, NO SADDLES. When Donald Weisert (standing second from left) was at Chernofski, the Japanese bombed Dutch Harbor.

FROM 1942-44, I was in the Army and stationed on Umnak Island. While I was there, a request was made of the Army for volunteers to help shear sheep at Chernofski Sheep Ranch. I volunteered to go and helped Don Green, the ranch manager.

Among my Army papers, I recently found an old yellowed pay envelope made out to "Sheep Herder Townsend" from the War Department, for wages earned on the Chernofski Sheep Ranch.

—*Joe Townsend*
Clifton, Texas

SHEEP HERDER? When Joe Townsend volunteered to help at Chernofski, he earned wages from wool.

ONE TIME, a freighter came to Chernofski with supplies, and the captain decided to dock the ship without the help of a tug.

The wind was blowing toward the land. It pushed the vessel, causing it to hit the dock right on the end. That ship plowed along for about 30 yards, grinding dock lumber all the way. I can still hear the sound of those big pilings as they were snapping off. —*Reginald Strout, Brewer, Maine*

MY UNIT was one of the first to go west of Unalaska Island during World War II.

My diary contains this description of the Aleutian winds, as written by a Lieutenant Miller, of my unit:

"Can you imagine men out on a great barren, walking against a 100-mph wind that rips the grass out by its roots; that blows marble-sized chunks of snow horizontally without dropping them; a wind of fits and starts, of gust and gusto, that drives your words back into your teeth before you can utter them, freezes your breath on your parka and beard, and ices your eyelashes shut and frost your cheeks; a wind that rips a tent from side to side in 10 minutes and drives sleet right through a piece of 26-ounce canvas?" — *Willie Stubbs, Little Rock, Arkansas*

FROM 1944 to 1946, I was stationed on Umnak. It was monotonous, but we did have some excitement.

Mt. Tulic decided to become an active volcano after lying dormant for hundreds of years. The eruptions lasted 9 or 10 days.

Joe Louis, the heavyweight champ, was also in the Army. He gave an exhibition bout at our camp, and later on, I asked to have a picture taken with him. I was only 5-foot-4, so we

ONLY THE LONELY. How could anyone be lonely with this happy staff of the Umnak Service Club waiting to serve them? Anthony Zembrello supplied the photo.

looked like Mutt and Jeff. While posing for the picture, Joe looked down at me and asked, "Are you standing in a hole?"
—*Anthony Zembrello, Rensselaer, New York*

OVERMATCHED. There was no contest in the height department when Anthony Zembrello posed next to heavyweight champ Joe Louis.

AS A MEMBER of a USO camp show unit, I toured the Aleutians entertaining military personnel. Since there were so few women in the islands at that time, we four girls created a sensation wherever we went.

We flew into Dutch Harbor and were hoisted onto a barge with a cargo lift.

A short trip later, we arrived at Chernofski. We went to a ranch house and had some coffee with the couple who lived there.

The host and hostess had a large collection of pebbles from the beach, and they invited each of us to choose some. I took a few green stones, which proved to be jasper. I later had them cut, polished and set in silver. Today, I have a bracelet and earrings to remind me.

—Alice Mack Rowe
Los Angeles, California

CHEEK TO CHEEK. Alice Mack Rowe, singing a duet with Willard Reese, and accompanied by Eleanor Weller, has fond memories of Chernofski.

A Modern Fable

It was sad to read the epilogue to your book. Randall left to become a longshoreman and married, while Chuck chose the life of a fisherman. Where does that leave you and Milt? Do you intend to operate the ranch with hired help? With Milt's hip difficulties, you can't chase cattle and sheep with a tractor.

—John Brosky
Pittsburgh, Pennsylvania

TOGETHERNESS. Milt and I enjoy working together, no matter the task.

JOHN, who just underwent major heart surgery, knows how painful and frustrating it is to slow down before you want to. In answer to his question, and to sum up our lives and expectations as I end this book, I wrote a little "fairy tale" describing one of our most difficult, yet satisfying, summers:

ONCE UPON A TIME, a little old man and his crippled wife lived on a sheep ranch in the Aleutian Islands.

Their children had grown up and gone. The shepherds had all left to fish crabs for rich wages. All they had left were the sheep.

Every day the little old man looked at them through his field glasses. They got shaggier and shaggier. One day he turned to his crippled wife.

"We must shear the sheep," he said.

"Old man, you are crazy," she answered.

The little old man shrugged and limped out to the barn on his crutches.

The next morning, he started his track machine, put his

ON TRACK. Even if he can't walk or ride a horse, Milt can get a day's work done with the tracked Ferret.

SHEAR DELIGHT. Although he would have sheared all the sheep himself, Milt got help.

SHOVE OFF! Twelve miles of ocean travel in a tiny boat are no concern for Milt. He gets around just fine in this craft and slightly larger dory.

crutches in the back and called his dogs. At the last minute, his crippled wife climbed on the back and held on with one hand.

They bounced over the tundra all day, but the sheep were too fast for them. The sheep heard the machine and ran away. But the little old man did not stop.

He drove to the farthest point of his sheep range and turned around. The engine scared his sheep. They ran toward the barns. But it was a long way and his machine sputtered and ran out of gas. He had to walk 2 miles home on crutches. All the sheep escaped.

His crippled wife screamed and wept.

The little old man only shrugged and limped on.

The next morning, the little old man started his grown son's three-wheeler and put a can of gasoline on the handlebars. He called his dogs. At the last minute, his crippled wife climbed on the back and held on with one hand. The little old man drove to his track machine and filled the gas tank, then off they went to find the scattered sheep.

They were everywhere. The little old man and his crippled wife could not gather them. All they had to show for 2 days of hard work was one injured ewe and a lamb who couldn't run.

His wife screamed and wept. "You are insane," she said.

The little old man shrugged.

The next morning, the little old man started his track machine and called his dogs. At the last minute, his crippled wife said, "Catch my horse." And she got in the saddle and held the reins with one hand.

Again they went to the farthest point and turned around with the sheep in front of them. They gathered 200 sheep and put them in the barn.

The next day, the little old man sheared 40 sheep.

His crippled wife said, "You're killing yourself."

The little old man didn't say anything.

The next day, the little old man sheared 45 sheep...and the next day and the next. His crippled wife helped hold them down with one hand.

On the fifth day, a man from the next island called on the

radio and said, "If you will come get me, I will shear your sheep."

The little old man said, "Yes."

He got his boat into the water, His crippled wife screamed and wept. "It's 12 miles of open sea."

The little old man said, "I'll be careful."

And he was.

After all 500 sheep were sheared, the little old man took the young man back across the 12 miles of open water in his fast little boat. On the opposite shore, they shook hands.

"You are amazing," the young man said.

The little old man shrugged.

At breakfast the next morning, the little old man said, "Our coal shed is almost empty."

"I know," his crippled wife replied. "Maybe one of our sons will come help."

"They have their own lives," the little old man answered.

"We can't do it alone," his crippled wife cried. "The coal pile is across the bay. We aren't strong enough anymore."

The little old man didn't say anything. He went to the barn and chopped kindling.

NUMEROUS BITUMINOUS. Milt built this screen for sifting coal left by the military. Milt's sifting removes rocks from the coal, then he bags and hauls the fuel by hand.

NOT ALL ALONE. *Milt and I will never be the only ones living here on the ranch—not as long as I keep adopting pets like this bum lamb.*

The next day, the little old man got into his boat and went across the bay. He shoveled coal all day, but only filled the sacks half full. He dragged 50 sacks down the beach to the boat, wrestled them over the side and took them home.

His crippled wife screamed and wept. "You're killing yourself."

The little old man shrugged.

The next day, he filled 60 sacks...and the next day and the next. His crippled wife helped him drag them down the beach with one hand.

After the coal shed was full, the little old man said to his cripple wife, "Winter is almost here. The house needs a new roof."

"I agree," she said. "Tomorrow we will start on it."

The little old man smiled.

The moral of the story is: Never underestimate the power of a little old man!

GREAT TEAM. From feeding a lamb by bottle to running our diesel power plant, Milt can do just about anything. Together, we make a very good team.